Endorsements

The Missional Journey is a practical guide for churches looking to put their faith into action. Read this book if you're serious about having a powerful incarnational impact in your community.
　　　　　　 – Darren Adwalpalker, Pastor/Multiethnic Church Planter

For years we have been challenged to change the score card for ministry effectiveness. Bob not only changes the score card, he gives us the new rules for the game.
　　　　　　 – Dr. Steve Ogne, Church Resource Ministries

What excites me most about ministry is to see lives impacted and transformed by Jesus. *The Missional Journey* is a practical resource that clarifies the path to follow in order to fulfill our real purpose: to be Jesus disciples who love God and serve his Kingdom.
　　　　　　 – Yolanda Barquera, Christian coach and consultant, Mexico

The Missional Journey is well-grounded, field-tested, and action-oriented. If you want to really engage the world as a missional leader, keep this book close when you're drawing up plans and taking next steps.
　　　　　　 – Randy Shaw, Teaching Pastor at Missio and Director at
　　　　　　　 nwchurchplanting.org

As someone longing to see the congregations and clergy of our Diocese become more fruitful, I am delighted with *The Missional Journey*. Bob Logan gives concrete, specific help to those who are eager to engage their world the way Jesus did.
　　　　　　 – Mary Maggard Hays, Clergy and congregational development,
　　　　　　　 Anglican Diocese of Pittsburgh

Bob Logan, one of the fathers of the modern day church planting movement, along with Dave DeVries, takes us to the heart of what the missional journey is all about – the Kingdom of God, discipleship and multiplying movements.
　　　　　　 – JR Woodward, Co-founder of the Ecclesia Network, author
　　　　　　　 of *Creating a Missional Culture*

For too long, the church in North America has failed to make the connection between evangelism, church planting, missional living, sacrificial service and authentic discipleship. *The Missional Journey* does just that.
　　　　　　 – Rev. Dr. Craig S. Williams, Associate, Presbyterian Centers for
　　　　　　　 New Church Innovation - PCUSA

Conversations about what's "missional" abound, but Bob Logan and Dave DeVries have moved the ball down the field with this eminently practical book on how missionality works out in practice. This volume is biblical, relevant, and comprehensive.
> – Sam Metcalf, President, CRM-US

The Missional Journey is task theology at its finest. This is no ordinary missional book. It's a missional manual, written by an outstanding practitioner who has been on the journey and guiding other sojourners for decades.
> – Dr. John L. Amstutz, Foursquare Missions International consultant

Bob does it again! In his masterful way he has taken the hot, but often misunderstood, topic of being missional and has made it both understandable and practical for anyone who is on or wants to be on the missional journey.
> – Dana Allin, Synod Executive, ECO: A Covenant Order of Evangelical Presbyterians

Bob Logan is rare: he manages to be conceptual and comprehensive while giving us lots of practical, down-to-earth help. Bob an encouraging friend, coach and wise sounding board. I recommend *The Missional Journey* with the confidence that he will successfully help get you where you are called to go.
> – Todd Hunter, Anglican Bishop, founder *Churches for the Sake of Others*, author of *Giving Church Another Chance*

In *The Missional Journey*, Bob clearly identifies the stages by which disciples are multiplied into movements. He punctuates his insights with inspiring stories taken from real situations.... Bob is spot on.
> – Mark Fields, Director of Global and Intercultural Ministry, Vineyard USA

I've read a lot books on ministry but this might be the best. It's a delight to see this wonderful synthesis and development of years of experience and research. Your ministry won't be the same.
> – Dr. Robert Acker, Sr. Pastor, Community Baptist Church

I first became aware of Bob Logan's work as young pastor eager to move beyond the basics of the church growth movement. I continue to learn from Bob in his latest work as he leads us forward in the vital nature of discipleship in the missional church movement.
> – Mike Slaughter, Pastor, Ginghamsburg Church

Most missional leaders know their mission. They have some understanding of their vision. They're sketchy on how to get there. What I appreciate about Bob Logan is his ability to help missional leaders turn vision into reality.
> – Rev. Tom De Vries, D.Min. General Secretary, Reformed Church in America

With biblical insight and Holy Spirit-driven truths, Bob outlines a present-day missional approach to ministry based on how Jesus himself lived incarnationally. A must-read for any individual engaged in transformational ministry.
> – Jamie and Alissa Shattenberg, Red Island Restoration, Madagascar

Finally, a missional book that leans more toward the practical than the theoretical!
> – Robin Dugall, Professor and pastor

If you simply want theory, this book is not for you. Here you will find a biblical theology of the Kingdom with specific and tangible tools for fulfilling the great commission in your city.
> – Dr. John Jackson, President of William Jessup University and Leadership Author and Speaker, www.drjohnjackson.com

Bob Logan once again balances thoughtful reflection with pragmatic principles. Chronicling *The Missional Journey* from biblical theology to multiplying movements, this book touches on issues at the heart of God.
> – Dr. Gary Reinecke, Ministry Coach & Trainer at InFocus

The true value of Bob Logan's book, *The Missional Journey*, can only be discovered in its application. It is a must-use resource for all of us serious about engaging God's mission in this world.
> – Takeshi Takazawa, Vice President for Strategic Engagement, AsianAccess

Logan once again takes the complex and makes it accsessable to all, grounding everything in transferable principles. *The Missional Journey* gives us a consistent, simple, yet profound understanding of what it means to be a 'missional' church.
> – Jeannette Slater, Ministry Coach

The Missional Journey contains both key holistic principles and very practical self-coaching and action steps.
> – Rob Gill, CRM Leadership Developer and Coach, Asia

When Bob Logan has something to say, the rest of us have something to hear. With *The Missional Journey*, Bob circles back to what is foundational in our faith-- a lived-out missional life. I'm not one of those people who says "profound" very often, but I'm saying it here. As he has done for decades, Bob Logan supplies a workable guide that inspires us to effectively expand our reach.
> – Tom Nebel, Director of church planting, Converge Worldwide

With years of practical experience and wisdom, Bob Logan stays on the cutting edge of issues that deeply affect the church. We have applied the principles of this book in our church to help us find ways to engage our culture and reorient the mindset of this body of believers.
> – Keith Shields, Church Planter, Pastor, and Missional Coach, Vancouver, BC

Endorsements continued in the back of the book

The Missional Journey

Multiplying disciples and churches that transform the world

by Robert E. Logan
with Tara Miller
commentary by Dave DeVries

Published by ChurchSmart Resources

We are an evangelical Christian publisher committed to producing excellent products at affordable prices to help church leaders accomplish
effective ministry in the areas of church planting, church growth, church
renewal and leadership development.

For a free catalog of our resources call 1-800-253-4276.
Visit us at **www.ChurchSmart.com**

Cover design by: Julie Becker
Graphics and layout by: Julia Michaud
Edited by: Carl Simmons

ISBN: 978-1-936812-01-1

The Missional Journey

Multiplying disciples and churches that transform the world

Contents

Foreword

In 1990 I was a rookie pastor, fresh out of seminary, leading a struggling church in the eastern suburbs of Greater Los Angeles. My denomination tagged me to start a church planting work in our area, which had not been happening in a very long time. I knew enough to select a few motivated leaders to join me, but that was all I knew.

We heard of a training on starting new churches that was being conducted by an experienced church planter named Bob Logan, so the first official act of this group was to go to this training. We began a missional journey that day which has led us all over the world.

There were about 60 people at the training event from a variety of denominations. It was held at the church that Bob had started, which also happened to be just a couple blocks down the street from my own church property. We went with a desire to plant churches and no idea how to make it happen. Bob shared the riches of his experience and current learning.

We bought in and signed up to be a part of his new strategy, which was called the New Church Incubator (NCI). Little did we know that we were actually signing up to be part of a grand experiment that all of us would learn from for many years to come. What we thought was a finished plan was actually the first step of a long and fruitful missional journey. The NCI became a model for us and eventually birthed the Greenhouse movement and many other ideas shaping the church today.

The initial NCI training that day was helpful and got us started; it also got us connected to Bob and his partner Steve Ogne, another outstanding coach. Soon our group had a team of church planters that were meeting monthly in our own NCI and Bob and I began to work together on something we called the Pastor Factory (yes, this was before we became organic).

From these early days of experimentation and learning we developed a Profile Assessment System, the Life Transformation Groups, the Mentoring2Multiply System, and eventually the Greenhouse. Bob also introduced us to *Natural Church Development*, by Christian Schwarz, which was a seed of many new ideas propelling us toward organic church.

These days were full of learning. Bob and I made breakthroughs in leadership development under the mentoring of George Patterson and eventually we came up with a concept called Leadership Farm Systems, which was published under the title *Raising Leaders for the Harvest* (yes we began to think more organically by this time). Ten years later we coauthored *Beyond Church Planting*.

Bob has been a mentor to me, and a friend. We have learned from one another through the years and I am honored to be able to write this foreword for the man who wrote the foreword to my own first book, *Cultivating a Life for God*.

Bob Logan is well-known for his work and his writings. He is a coach, speaker and strategist. Being a true introvert, however, few have come to know him well as a man, and I feel that needs to be corrected. So I will share with you here what I have learned about this man. It's true that Bob has taught me a lot of things about church planting, coaching, and even consulting, but in this foreword I wish to share the things I have learned most from Bob. which you cannot find printed on the pages of this book.

One thing I can tell you about Bob is that he truly is a genius. Bob is actually a mad scientist of sorts. Trained as a chemist who then went into church planting, he is always willing to experiment and try new things. He's willing to put some catalysts in a pot, stir and see what emerges. He observes with a scientist's patience, and he is very calculating as he writes everything down in his IBM ThinkPad for future reference.

Bob is great at observing and evaluating what he sees– especially people. He knows when he sees something good even if others do not see it yet. Bob's life is marked by quality people that were unknown when he met them but now are making significant impact in the Kingdom of God.

I have been blessed to be the guinea pig on more than a few of his wild experiments and I am a better man for it. I didn't always find the cheese at the end of the puzzle but we learned a lot together. There are very few books that I have written which do not mention Bob at some point because his influence is all over my life. Often his words come out of my mouth and vice versa. Such is the way of learning together in a truly effective ongoing think tank. I know that I owe much to his keen eye and willingness to take a chance on an unproven young leader with crazy ideas.

Bob is a man who thinks out ahead of most people. He is also a risk taker who will bank everything on a risky experiment. As times change Bob stays out in front, an important testimony to his leadership approach. I have seen him leave past success behind to embrace the risk of future ideas… and potential failure. This speaks to his courageous faith. It is easy to transition from failure, but to do so from huge success is the kind of bold leader I can follow.

I have, on several occasions, watched Bob abandon ideas that were seen as success in the past to learn new ideas for a better future. I was so proud the day that Bob and Janet set out to start churches again in a more organic way reaching out to the broken people living on the margins of life in Los Angeles. He did this after years of being the "go-to" expert on more traditional church planting methods. Oh that more would also follow this example.

Many people get an idea and publish it as quickly as they can. These may be thought leaders, but the people who buy the books end up being the proof of their idea, whether good or bad. I learned from Bob not to publish something until it has been proven in more than one context. As a result of his example I have restrained from publishing things until I can point to real examples and I believe it has made my books far better and longer lasting. There is a word for this: integrity. I am grateful for learning this from Bob, and again, I wish more would follow his lead.

There are a few of us that have worked closely with Bob over the years and now have influence deep and wide in the Kingdom of God. It wouldn't do well to call us "Logan-ites," but we all know where our influence began. When we are together recounting stories there is one common theme that seems to emerge. We all have seen Bob step forward at appropriate times with a bold message of uncompromising truth spoken with clarity and no regard for political correctness.

We call him the "thundering prophet" at those moments because when it happens we all know that it wasn't Bob speaking to us, it was God speaking through a yielded and fearless vessel. I think those are some of my fondest memories of this man and I welcome him to speak truth to me whenever His Lord gives him that command. I have tried to emulate that quality in my own life.

All of these qualities have one common trait that is indeed important to you as you read this book: Bob is a learner. Learners make the best teachers for obvious reasons. This book is full of a lifetime of learning from a mad scientist who has conducted many trials and has some proven ideas to share with you now. You will not find fluff in this book; the thundering prophet has little patience for fluff. With a strict economy of words he will get to the point quickly, explain it sufficiently yet without doing all the thinking for you. Then Bob will challenge you to think through the application in your own environment. All of this is classic Logan and makes this book a valuable addition to your own learning.

On that morning in the early nineties when I heard Bob Logan for the first time, he brought up on stage a young potential church planter who had yet to do anything. They ran him through a mock church planter assessment to demonstrate for us how a good assessment is conducted. That young man passed the assessment and started a church in the Lake Castaic area of Los Angeles. He is another example of how Bob spots talent before others and invests in people that will eventually make an impact. That church planter later went on to become a strategic missional thinker, author, and personal friend. His name is Dave DeVries and he has added some key insights throughout this book from his own rich experience, making this a deeper and richer resource that goes further than the 180 pages would seem to indicate.

Who could have imagined what eggs were to be hatched from that New Church Incubator back in the early nineties? That gathering ended up birthing a lot, for multiple generations, and we all owe Bob Logan our gratitude. As life goes ripping past us and our hairline starts thinning while our waistline thickens, it is easy to not take a moment and give honor and respect where it is due.

I know it is traditional for a foreword to speak about the subject of the book. Forgive me this unconventional moment as I have shared with you what I have learned from Bob that you cannot find on these pages... but are between every line.

Thanks Bob. Your example lives on in us "Logan-ites" that you have released in this world.

The missional journey continues...

Neil Cole
Long Beach, CA
2013

To Janet,

who not only is my lifelong partner,
but who embodies the missional quality of life
that is written about in this book.

Introduction

It's all connected

There are plenty of books about discipleship and about Christian living. Likewise, there are plenty of books about the church, about leading groups, and even about church planting. There are very few books that are about all of these things—and how the pieces fit together.

But that's what *The Missional Journey: multiplying disciples and churches that transform the world* is all about. Everything is crammed into that subtitle: making disciples, starting churches, multiplying at every level, and making a difference in the world around us. Together, all of this adds up to a renewed vision for what the church could look like, from the grassroots up.

From handing someone a cup of cold water to the great multitude standing around the throne praising God… it's all connected. In fact, the pieces are inseparable. Try launching a movement without living as Jesus did. Try leading a missional community without making any disciples. Try reaching those who don't know Jesus without engaging in service to the world around you. None of it works without the rest of it.

Too often we compartmentalize our faith, separating serving from worship, or discipleship from church

Here's the problem - there are church planters all across the country that are failing to put the pieces together. That's why there are small groups that have never experienced seeing one of their members become a follower of Jesus. That's why there are churches that only serve the needs of their members. And the reality is—it doesn't work. This book will show you not only why "it's all connected," but show you how to put all the pieces together.

- Dave

planting. This book is about how all these pieces fit together; if you remove one, the whole structure crumbles. The purpose of this book is to provide a broad map of the missional journey—and then equip you, the missional leader, to help people along each stage of the way.

For those with a broad vision for making a difference for the Kingdom, this book will provide a bird's-eye view of the finished puzzle. You'll see the broader implications of implementing the missional journey across multiple communities. In the final chapter, we specifically address network leaders who oversee multiple faith communities.

However, the primary reader for this book is the missional church planter. As you organize your thinking around the missional journey, one thing you'll begin to recognize is the outsized influence of planters who are pioneering new ministries. These missional leaders are serving at the point of maximum leverage, working directly with a group of people living on mission together. Missional church planters most directly impact what happens on the ground; therefore, they're in the best position to raise up more leaders and have the broadest impact.

If you're a network leader, you might be tempted to jump to the last chapter. If you do, you're in danger of missing how everything fits together. If you decide to read the last chapter now, please come back and read the rest too!

- Dave

Executive or regional leaders face the considerable challenge of trying to implement top-down change. Individuals at the grassroots level, on the other hand, often have trouble creating enough traction or momentum to get going. Both of those roles are certainly important, and will be addressed to a degree in this book. But if you're launching a new ministry that meets the culture on its own turf, consider yourself in the sweet spot. You can radiate the change from there in both directions.

So as I write, I'll be primarily addressing missional church planters and missional leaders pioneering new ministries. That's who we need to empower if we want to see the widespread change of a movement take hold—because that's where the missional journey can make the most powerful impact.

The journey guides are intended to be used with your team or coach to process the material in each chapter. Don't rush through the reading. Stop at each journey guide and take time to reflect, and to decide on action steps.

- Dave

You may have noticed the running commentary in the shaded boxes—that's Dave DeVries. He'll be adding his thoughts in this way throughout the book, and he helped shape the "journey guides" at the end of each chapter. Dave is a church planter, coach, and missional leader, and is partnering with me to bring you a whole set of training resources that will follow. This book is just the starting point in resourcing missional church planters. We'll be continuing to learn from the experiences of others and will share the fruit of our findings with you.

You'll hear much more from Dave as we partner together on the follow-up training materials. For now, just sit back and enjoy his contributions and insights here. And as you read through this book, add your own commentary—that's what margins are for.

Starting points and structure

As I began writing this book, I was well aware that we don't need another book on theory. Theory is important, and there are a lot of great books out there on missional ministry. But as I've worked in this field for a while now, the consistent missing piece is a holistic process for implementation. How do we actually go about doing all of this?

We are still in need of an implementation strategy that's based on clear biblical thinking. I have a lot of experience with implementation, both in my own ministry over the years and out of the coaching work I do with other ministry leaders. Many of my insights are gleaned from that experience.

However, when writing about the missional journey, I felt the need to start with a clean slate. A lot of people talk about "missional" ministry, but what does it really mean? Therefore, I began this book not by looking at other books or theories from the missional movement but simply by looking at scripture to see what the Bible had to say about the Kingdom of God—about the church, and about what it means to be a disciple of Jesus

Technically speaking, the word "missional" is an adjective that comes from the word missionary. It describes a person or group of people who have been sent "on mission" by Jesus. Missional living is about living on mission. Missional activities are the focus of your life as you seek to fulfill the mission of Jesus.

— Dave

and to live as he lived. I wanted to start fresh from the original source, to see what it looks like. The goal was not to create a comprehensive theology, but rather a bare-bones one. What are the most basic truths—the things that virtually everyone who calls themselves followers of Jesus can buy into? What are the essentials that we can agree on and say, "Yes. This is what it means to follow Jesus. This is what it means to be the church"?

For my purposes here, I'm defining "missional" as any person (or group of people) who is focused on living in accordance with the great commandment and great commission.

Consequently, the first part of this book is basic theology. What is the Kingdom of God? The gospel? A disciple? What do gatherings of disciples look like as we live together? What is the church supposed to do? How do we live like Jesus lived? How do we make more disciples? I started with scripture, distilled principles, and was pleased to find similarities with much of the other missional thinking already out there.

If you're looking for a program to implement in your church plant—so that it all of a sudden becomes "missional" - you're not going to find it here. In fact, it doesn't exist. But you will discover both missional principles and practical processes you can implement immediately as you read.

Focus first on how you're living out what you're reading. Then, it will be much easier to help those on mission with you to join you in your missional journey.

— Dave

The second part of this book focuses on how to implement those principles—from engaging the culture around us to creating multiplying movements of Jesus-followers. How can we create processes that are principle-based, yet not programmatic? Processes that are flexible enough to be adapted to specific contexts, and responsive to the leadings of the Holy Spirit?

We'll look at how the missional journey works itself out along four related journeys:

- Engaging culture
- Forming missional communities
- Developing leadership
- Multiplying movements

Each of these journeys multiplies itself, and each branches off into the next. All four, taken together, make up the missional journey.

The structure of this book reflects how I've always worked and written: starting with my experiences and with scripture, field-testing ideas in working with others, trying to live into them, distilling principles, then designing a process for implementing those principles into a variety of ministry contexts.

This book was designed to be read and processed together with other people. Therefore, I encourage you to work through this book with your team, especially if you're leading a missional community or in the early stages of planting a church. Engaging the material together will prove helpful in working through the concepts and getting everyone on the same page. Take time, particularly, to pray together. Any missional endeavor is conceived and birthed in prayer. We need the power of the Holy Spirit to move forward together in productive directions.

My vision for many years now has been to help resource church planters to do the work of the Kingdom. I am continually in the process of developing new tools and templates to help you accomplish your vision more effectively. This book serves as a launching point for more resources to come—specifically *The Missional Church Planters Toolkit* (www.missionaltoolkit.com), which will provide hand-on resources for church planters at each stage of the process.

Chapter 1

The Kingdom of God

You may have noticed that the first few chapters are devoted to what are generally considered theological issues: the Kingdom of God, the role of the incarnation, and the meaning of the church.

An obvious question is raised—namely: Why do we need to think about all this? Because the church is the gospel lived out. Beliefs translate to actions; actions translate to identity. What we believe directly informs how we choose to live and how we invest our lives.

What did Jesus tell us to do? He told us to make disciples. That is the core mission we've been charged with. Disciples make up, and move forward, the Kingdom of God. Any attempt at making disciples, therefore, must be grounded in a clear understanding of the Kingdom of God. Here we'll take a broad sweep of the Kingdom of God through scripture, and draw some conclusions about what it means.

> *Jesus never started a local church or commanded anyone to start churches. Jesus made disciples and instructed his disciples to make disciples. Churches are the natural outcome of disciples making disciples. Therefore, don't be dreaming of how you're going to start a church as you read this book. Instead, start dreaming of how you're going to obey Jesus by making disciples who make disciples. If you do this well, you'll find churches will be multiplied as you go.*
> *- Dave*

That said, the purpose of this chapter—and this first section—is not primarily theological. The purpose is to help you process together how you are living out the Kingdom of God. How are you incorporating that essential Kingdom

These are great questions! The temptation as you read a book and come across a good question is to think, "That's a good question"... then just keep on reading. My challenge to you is to resist this temptation. When you find a good question—or list of questions—take the time to consider them. Moving too quickly through this book can actually hinder you and your team from becoming truly effective.

— Dave

DNA into your ministry? What parts are missing? Which parts need more emphasis? What do you really believe about God, community, and the church? By working through this chapter with your group or team, you can help people see their roles in the larger kingdom of God, both corporately and individually.

Helping each individual see the bigger picture is essential. Think of the story about the two men working. You approach one man working out in the hot sun and ask him, "What are you doing?" He responds, "I am laying bricks." You then move to the other man, who appears to be doing the same thing, and ask him the same question. His response? "I'm building a cathedral. It probably won't be finished in my lifetime, but someday it will be a great monument for God."

Perspective makes all the difference. How can you help the other people on your group or team to see that what they're doing and how they are serving is part of something so much bigger than just their individual efforts? Each contribution to the Kingdom of God matters—and together, they form something greater than the sum of their parts.

The church is not the end. We need to understand that the church is the means to get to the end goal. The end goal is the Kingdom of God and the glory of God. We must take the time to understand how the church connects to the Kingdom of God.

— Dave

When working within the area of incarnational and missional ministry, it becomes important to be able to articulate some coherent understanding of the Kingdom of God. Throughout church history, people have used the phrase "Kingdom of God" for vastly different purposes. Although we're sure our definitions here will fall far short of the ultimate reality, at the same time we hope they will speak clearly to the vastly diverse people who consider themselves followers of Jesus, and inform the way we choose to live. Rather than trying to outline what's different and unique about the beliefs expressed here, our hope is to state the most obvious, most basic assumptions about the Kingdom of God that the vast majority of believers would be able to come together around and agree upon.

Any review of the Kingdom of God must begin with scripture. Most of the rest of this chapter is structured around the passages that speak most directly to the subject. From each of those passages, we'll draw some conclusions about how to understand the Kingdom of God.

Announcing the Kingdom of God (Mark 1:14–15)

After John was put in prison, Jesus went into Galilee, proclaiming the good news of God. "The time has come," he said. "The kingdom of God has come near. Repent and believe the good news!"

Earlier John the Baptist had announced the coming of Jesus. Now Jesus is saying that the time has come. He announces the good news that the Kingdom of God has come near. In a biblical theology, the Kingdom—not just our own salvation—becomes the centerpiece of scripture. What we usually think of as the gospel, the way of human salvation, is just one part of an even larger story. And as we see from the next passage, this story is preached holistically—with both words and works.

The good news (Luke 4:16–21)

He went to Nazareth, where he had been brought up, and on the Sabbath day he went into the synagogue, as was his custom. He stood up to read, and the scroll of the prophet Isaiah was handed to him. Unrolling it, he found the place where it is written:

"The Spirit of the Lord is on me,
because he has anointed me to proclaim good news to the poor.
He has sent me to proclaim freedom for the prisoners
and recovery of sight for the blind,

to set the oppressed free, to proclaim the year of the Lord's favor."

Then he rolled up the scroll, gave it back to the attendant and sat down. The eyes of everyone in the synagogue were fastened on him. He began by saying to them, "Today this scripture is fulfilled in your hearing."

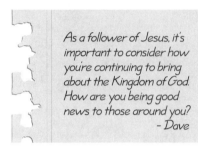

As a follower of Jesus, it's important to consider how you're continuing to bring about the Kingdom of God. How are you being good news to those around you?
- Dave

John the Baptist first announced the coming of the Kingdom of God (Matt. 3:1–3, Luke 16:16) by quoting the prophet Isaiah. Likewise, Jesus chose to inaugurate his public ministry by quoting Isaiah 61—an announcement of good news, justice, and the release from captivity and oppression. Not only that, but he proclaimed that his arrival was what was bringing this vision about—he would accomplish it.

This is how Jesus understood the coming Kingdom, and how he announced it at the beginning of his ministry. As a result, any later concept of Kingdom ministry must incorporate practical service to "the least of these"—the poor, the prisoners, the blind, the oppressed. That was Jesus' expectation as he inaugurated the Kingdom of God. This passage defines the good news that he brought: not only the gospel of his incarnation, death and resurrection, but also the accompanying release from captivity, freedom for the oppressed, sight for the blind, and hope for the poor. The good news was, and is, "both/and."

Thy Kingdom come (Matt. 6:9–10)

"This, then, is how you should pray:
"'Our Father in heaven,
hallowed be your name,
your Kingdom come,
your will be done,
on earth as it is in heaven.

As God's people, we are committed to God's reign in the here and now, in anticipation of the rule of the Kingdom of God that is to come. Jesus is the king of this Kingdom. Even as Jesus inaugurated the Kingdom of God with his first coming, the Kingdom will not come in all its fullness until he returns as king.

But to what degree is the Kingdom being lived in the here and now in the meantime? That's the issue being addressed here in the Lord's Prayer. What are we doing to show the Kingdom right here, right now… on earth as it is in heaven? That's the good news of the gospel: It has come, and it will come. Both/and.

The gospel

The word *gospel* has been used throughout history in many different ways and is seeing a resurgence today. The term brings to mind associations as diverse as the evangelistic crusades of Billy Graham, the four spiritual laws, and a type of music. *Gospel* (euaggelion in koine Greek) means "good news." What good news? What did Jesus have in mind when he said, "And the *gospel* must first be preached to all nations?" (Mark 13:10, emphasis mine)

Any search for the meaning of gospel must begin with scripture. The first use of the word gospel in scripture occurs when Jesus quotes from Isaiah at the inauguration of his ministry, in our earlier passage from Luke 4:16–21. Jesus seems to have picked up on Isaiah's use of the term good news, or gospel, and used it in a more specialized way. From this point on, Jesus uses the term gospel twice in Matthew and five times in Mark. In every one of those cases, gospel seems to be referring to verbal content—a message that is to be preached. For example, *"Truly I tell you, wherever this gospel is preached throughout the world, what she has done will also be told, in memory of her"* (Matt. 26:13).

Jesus seemed to use the word *gospel* synonymously with *good news*, and often linked it with the *Kingdom of God:*

> *"And this gospel of the kingdom will be preached in the whole world as a testimony to all nations, and then the end will come" (Matt. 24:14).*

> *"The time has come," he said, "The Kingdom of God has come near. Repent and believe the good news!" (Mark 1:15).*

But he said, "I must proclaim the good news of the kingdom of God to the other towns too, for that is why I was sent" (Luke 4:43).

That's the message Jesus brought us—and the message he commands us to bring to the world: the gospel/good news of the Kingdom of God.

Usage of the term gospel picks up dramatically in the book of Acts, and continues in the epistles written by Paul and Peter. Gospel overwhelmingly appears in the context of a message to be preached. Typical usages in Acts include:

After they had further proclaimed the word of the Lord and testified about Jesus, Peter and John returned to Jerusalem, preaching the gospel in many Samaritan villages (Acts 8:25).

After much discussion, Peter got up and addressed them: "Brothers, you know that some time ago God made a choice among you that the Gentiles might hear from my lips the message of the gospel and believe (Acts 15:7).

The usage of *gospel* in the epistles continues to focus upon preaching the gospel, faith in the gospel as a means of salvation, and the gospel as a message:

He gave me the priestly duty of proclaiming the gospel of God, so that the Gentiles might become an offering acceptable to God, sanctified by the Holy Spirit (Rom. 15:16).

I am astonished that you are so quickly deserting the one who called you to live in the grace of Christ and are turning to a different gospel—which is really no gospel at all. Evidently some people are throwing you into confusion and are trying to pervert the gospel of Christ. But even if we or an angel from heaven should preach a gospel other than the one we preached to you, let them be under God's curse! (Gal. 1:6–8).

And you also were included in Christ when you heard the message of truth, the gospel of your salvation. When you believed, you were marked in him with a seal, the promised Holy Spirit (Eph. 1:13).

Yet we see hints that the apostles are broadening the usage of the term *gospel* beyond simply referencing the message of the life, death, and resurrection of Jesus as a means of salvation. The *gospel* is also something with power—something to be lived, something to be obeyed.

> *because our gospel came to you not simply with words but also with power, with the Holy Spirit and deep conviction. You know how we lived among you for your sake (1 Thess. 1:5).*

> *I became a servant of this gospel by the gift of God's grace given me through the working of his power (Eph. 3:7).*

> *For it is time for judgment to begin with God's household; and if it begins with us, what will the outcome be for those who do not obey the gospel of God? (1 Pet. 4:17).*

It's also interesting the written accounts of the life of Jesus (Matthew, Mark, Luke, and John) came to be known as *the gospels*. The gospel, then, is not simply a message; it's a story. It's the story of the life, death, and resurrection of Jesus. It's a story that comes with the power of the Holy Spirit. It's a story that is not just to be believed, but to be lived and shared.

That's the way we'll be using the term *gospel* in this book. When responded to, the gospel story has the power to change lives. It's the good news of forgiveness, the redemption of sin, transformation, sanctification, the resurrection of the body, and the coming of the Kingdom of God. What we're talking about is a spiritual reality that transcends language.

There it is—a great question. How are you to live out the gospel life? Don't rush on with the rest of the chapter yet. Consider: How are you, as a Jesus-follower, living out the gospel in your neighborhood?
— Dave

The real question, then, is: How we are to live out this kind of life?

The dream of the gospel

In 1963, Martin Luther King Jr. gave a brief, seventeen-minute speech
that changed the way people thought about racial relations in the United
States. Who would have thought an idea—a vision—could have such a
powerful impact? It didn't change things overnight, and plenty of things still
need to change; still, something shifted in the consciousness of a country
that day. People could see a different future that they couldn't see before,
and were motivated to work toward it. The power of dreaming isn't to be
underestimated.

> *And afterward,*
> *I will pour out my Spirit on all people.*
> *Your sons and daughters will prophesy,*
> *your old men will dream dreams,*
> *your young men will see visions.*
> *Even on my servants, both men and women,*
> *I will pour out my Spirit in those days.*
> *I will show wonders in the heavens*
> *and on the earth,*
> *blood and fire and billows of smoke (Joel 2:28–30).*

I have a dream of the gospel lived out.

I have a dream where churches are serving the world around us… not with an
eye toward ourselves, our own growth, our reputation, our benefit, but with
an eye outward: disinterested service that expects nothing in return. I have
a dream that we as the body of Christ would use our gifts, talents, time, and
money to serve as the hands and feet and voice of Jesus in the world—that we
would go where we are needed, help those in need in practical ways, and speak
up for the oppressed and the voiceless.

What if this vision were turned to reality? What would that look like? It
would look like food pantries, ministries to immigrants, prostitutes, prisoners,
the dying… the people the rest of society neglects. It would look like a church
no longer on the defensive, crumbling while guarding beliefs, but a church
open to conversation, willing to engage in dialogue without fear. It would look

like people listening for the voice of the Holy Spirit, with a willingness to act on those promptings when they come.

I have a dream where I see all the neighborhoods across my city of Los Angeles coming together to connect—first within themselves and then with each other. I have a dream that people would get to know their neighbors across the street and help them with their needs. From there, they would get to know their neighbor across the tracks. I have a dream that people would take the risks necessary to cross cultural and economic lines in an effort to understand "the other"—that we would put ourselves in the other person's shoes, instead of saying, "I would never be in that position." That communities of Jesus-followers would flower in every neighborhood, multiplying like dandelions. That the Holy Spirit would be at work in the very air.

What would it look like if that happened? We'd see the sharing of resources across neighborhood lines, and across color and culture lines. Churches and ministries would let one another—and the community—use their buildings. We'd see more partnerships to address problems. We'd see believers and unbelievers working side by side. We'd see a greater understanding for communities with problems that are different than our own. We'd feel a sense of ownership over "our" children rather than judgment or pity for "their" children. We'd start to recognize that we're actually on the same side.

Imagine the power of a gospel message that crosses these kinds of lines. Starting with something small, we would eventually see widespread societal transformation.

I have a dream that God would heal the wounds of the broken, and that he would use us to do it. That the emotional wounds of the fatherless, the neglected, and the abused would be healed—that the effects of generational sin would stop here, cleansed by the power of the Holy Spirit. I have a dream that churches would become places of forgiveness

Bob shared his dream of the gospel lived out. What's your dream? And in what ways does that dream resonate with what you've just read? Take a moment and write out your own dream of the gospel.

- Dave

rather than judgment. That the gospel would be shared not only in words, but also in deeds. That many believers would serve as listening ears for the hurting all around us. That the Spirit would heal and renew this generation in a way that would allow them not only to survive, but to live and thrive and give out from the love that God has showered on them.

I will make all things new

Too often we're afraid to dream for fear of not being able to make the dream reality. But something within us needs to dream, even when the reality is far down the road. And in the meantime, there are things we can do, decisions we can make, actions we can take. We may even see our dreams bridging into reality sooner than we expect. The change starts here, with us—and God promised he will make all things new:

> Then I saw "a new heaven and a new earth," for the first heaven and the first earth had passed away, and there was no longer any sea. I saw the Holy City, the new Jerusalem, coming down out of heaven from God, prepared as a bride beautifully dressed for her husband. And I heard a loud voice from the throne saying, "Look! God's dwelling place is now among the people, and he will dwell with them. They will be his people, and God himself will be with them and be their God. 'He will wipe every tear from their eyes. There will be no more death' or mourning or crying or pain, for the old order of things has passed away."
>
> He who was seated on the throne said, "I am making everything new!" Then he said, "Write this down, for these words are trustworthy and true."
>
> He said to me: "It is done. I am the Alpha and the Omega, the Beginning and the End. To the thirsty I will give water without cost from the spring of the water of life. Those who are victorious will inherit all this, and I will be their God and they will be my children (Rev. 21:1–7).

What will the Kingdom of God look like when it comes in all its fullness? No more sin, no more brokenness, no more crying or pain, for the old order of things has passed away. The Kingdom of God anticipates the new creation.

The removal of sin from the earth will be complete—just as complete as the removal of sin from the souls of people. Not only our souls, but our environments—both social and natural—will be restored. It will be a world where all is set right and things are as they were meant to be. Poverty, blindness, oppression, ecological destruction, and injustice will cease to exist. Instead, the light of God will shine into every corner of the new creation.

> *I did not see a temple in the city, because the Lord God Almighty and the Lamb are its temple. The city does not need the sun or the moon to shine on it, for the glory of God gives it light, and the Lamb is its lamp. The nations will walk by its light, and the kings of the earth will bring their splendor into it. On no day will its gates ever be shut, for there will be no night there (Rev. 21:22–25).*

That's the message of the gospel in full—and in its total fulfillment: Thy kingdom come, on earth as it is in heaven.

What is needed to live out the Kingdom of God? Disciples. People who live like Jesus lived. As those entrusted with revealing this Kingdom to others, we follow Jesus, imitate his ways, and try to live our lives as he lived his. We serve as the hands, feet, and voice of Jesus in the world around us. In doing so, we—as his disciples—participate in making the power of the God visible to others. Jesus invited others to taste and see the Kingdom of God, and he uses us as the means of expressing that spiritual reality to those around us.

Journey Guide: The Kingdom of God

Discussion questions: for you and your team

- What's your dream of the gospel lived out?
- How could you see the body of Christ using our various gifts, talents, money, and time to serve as the hands and feet of Jesus?
- How could you help those in need in practical ways?
- How could you speak up for the oppressed and voiceless?
- What are you hearing from the Holy Spirit?
- How are you willing to act on that?

Guided prayer: for you and your team

Take some time in group prayer to listen to the Holy Spirit. Commit to only asking questions of God, making no statements. Begin with this question: "What questions should we be asking you?" Allow for silence throughout your prayer time, as people listen for the voice of the Spirit.

Planning questions: for you and your coach

- What did you and your team hear from the Holy Spirit?
- How will what the Spirit's telling you further shape your vision?
- Take some time to write out your vision. Be as thorough as possible.
- What actions do you need to take to be obedient to what you've heard?
- What's your first step (or steps) in doing that?

To do list: action points to implement

Create your to-do list here. Start small. Here are some sample ideas are below to get you going:

1. Get to know your neighbors

- Introduce yourself, and share your story
- Discover their stories
- Find and meet needs they have (share resources)

2. Look for people living near you of different ethnicity, nationality, social/economic status

- Introduce yourself, and share your story
- Discover their stories
- Find and meet needs they have (share resources)

3. Develop community partnerships

- Discover what needs exist around you
- Look to see who's already working to meet those needs
- Seek to partner together with them

Listen + Serve + Forgive + Love + Repeat

To do list:

- _____

- _____

- _____

- _____

- _____

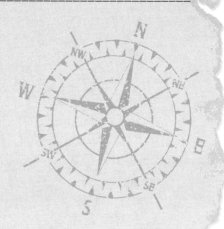

Chapter 2

What does incarnational ministry actually look like?

If this is the Kingdom of God, how will we live into it? How are we as disciples of Jesus to contribute to his Kingdom? What are disciples even supposed to look like? It's one thing to describe the Kingdom of God and gain a vision for it. It's quite another to figure out how to live it out.

> Living incarnationally literally means to make the word flesh (John 1:14). Therefore, it requires us to "be Jesus" to everyone, everywhere. It requires us to love like Jesus, serve like Jesus, care like Jesus, etc. Every Christian is sent by Jesus to be Jesus! Who will see Jesus in you today?
>
> - Dave

Much has been made lately of the phrase "living incarnationally." It's basically synonymous with living as a disciple of Jesus—living and loving as Jesus did. A bedrock passage for incarnational living is 1 John 2:5–6:

But if anyone obeys his word, love for God is truly made complete in them. This is how we know we are in him: Whoever claims to live in him must live as Jesus did.

We are to do the works that Jesus did. Jesus became incarnate to show us the gospel story; he lived on earth in a way that showed us what God is like. In the same way, we are to live in such a way as to show others what God is like. We are to live incarnationally—living as Jesus did and doing what he told us to do.

Although "living as Jesus did and doing what he told us to do" is a simple and accurate definition of "live incarnationally," it begs several important questions. How did Jesus actually live? What did he actually do? Which specific actions of his are we to imitate? What would those actions look like in our own very different cultural context? Given that we are not God, how can we really live like Jesus lived? Easier said than done, right?

In short: When we say we are to live incarnationally, what does that actually end up looking like in the real world?

In this chapter, we'll explore what it truly means to be a disciple. If we're going to live like Jesus and help others follow him, we need a clear picture of what a disciple looks like. If making disciples through incarnational ministry is our core goal, we need clarity in terms of what we are trying to produce. To that end, we'll address three things in this chapter:

1. How did Jesus live?
2. What did Jesus tell us to do?
3. How can we live that out, with all of our imperfections?

How did Jesus live?

I recently undertook a study of the gospels, with an eye toward what Jesus actually did during his time on earth. I wrote down the actions I saw Jesus taking and ended up with quite a list. Here are the seven principles that stood out to me:

- Principle #1: Staying connected with the Father
- Principle #2: Integrating into the culture
- Principle #3: Living with purpose
- Principle #4: Engaging authentically with others
- Principle #5: Serving the "least of these"
- Principle #6: Calling people to follow Jesus
- Principle #7: Cultivating others to live incarnationally

Principle #1: Staying connected with the Father

One principle I found when looking at the life of Jesus is that he stayed connected with the Father. That may sound simple and obvious, but it's amazing how quickly we lose sight of that over the course of day-to-day ministry— especially those of us who plan well. We can begin relying on the plan more than relying on the Father. If we're going to live incarnationally in the world around us, we're going to need to follow in the footsteps of Jesus, by staying connected with the Father like he did.

Jesus modeled for us his behavior of connecting with the Father:

> *Very early in the morning, while it was still dark, Jesus got up, left the house and went off to a solitary place, where he prayed (Mark 1:35).*

> *After he had dismissed them, he went up on a mountainside by himself to pray. Later that night, he was there alone… (Matt. 14:23).*

Jesus taught about the importance of connecting with the Father throughout John 15, where he told the parable of the vine and the branches, illustrating that connection with the Father is the key to ongoing fruitfulness. Jesus also acknowledged the importance of scripture and the state of the heart that comes about through connection with the Father:

> *Jesus replied, "You are in error because you do not know the scriptures or the power of God" (Matt. 22:29).*

> *Each tree is recognized by its own fruit. People do not pick figs from thornbushes, or grapes from briers. A good man brings good things out of the good stored up in his heart, and an evil man brings evil things out of the evil stored up in his heart. For the mouth speaks what the heart is full of (Luke 6:44–45).*

Ongoing connection with the Father is one area where we can follow the example of Jesus. If he needed that connection, how much more do we?

> *"I am the vine; you are the branches. If you remain in me and I in you, you will bear much fruit; apart from me you can do nothing" (John 15:5).*

Each of these principles, lived out in your life and the lives of your teammates, become habitual behaviors–habits of following Jesus. Consider your personal habits in each of these seven areas, as you read through them. Starting with Principle #1: What is your daily habit of staying connected with the Father?
– Dave

Principle #2: Integrating into the culture

Sometimes people think of Jesus as a religious person who taught religious sayings, isolated from the real pain and suffering of the world around him. But Jesus didn't live in an idealistic world of his own making, surrounded by people who agreed with him. He had relatives. He went to weddings and holiday festivals. He went to parties, where he met friends of friends. Jesus was a part of the culture he lived in.

Jesus didn't teach from afar. He lived personally and relationally among the people he ministered to. Some he knew well: He cried with them, laughed with them, ate with them, traveled with them. Sometimes we forget that there were others beyond the twelve disciples who traveled with Jesus.

> *After this, Jesus traveled about from one town and village to another, proclaiming the good news of the kingdom of God. The Twelve were with him, and also some women who had been cured of evil spirits and diseases: Mary (called Magdalene) from whom seven demons had come out; Joanna the wife of Chuza, the manager of Herod's household; Susanna; and many others. These women were helping to support them out of their own means (Luke 8:1–3).*

Other people he met for just a moment, but in that moment he touched them in a way that had lifelong impact:

> *Just then a woman who had been subject to bleeding for twelve years came up behind him and touched the edge of his cloak. She said to herself, "If I only touch his cloak, I will be healed." Jesus turned and saw her. "Take heart, daughter," he said, "your faith has healed you." And the woman was healed at that moment (Matt. 9:20–22).*

Think about the non-Christians with whom you interact on a regular basis. Picture their faces, and consider their relationship with Jesus. Unfortunately, a lot of Christians try to spend most of their time with Christian friends rather than spending time with those who need to meet Jesus. How can you develop a habit of spending time regularly with the people you know that don't yet follow Jesus?

– Dave

As we read through the gospels we can see example upon example of Jesus integrating into the culture and living his day-to-day life among the people he was called to. We see him attending parties, being invited into people's homes, teaching in the markets, being on the streets, fishing by the lake, attending in the temple courts. Jesus was where the people were. As one of the prophets recorded: "My dwelling place will be with them; I will be their

God, and they will be my people" (Ezek. 37:27).

We, too, need to live among people and be a real presence in their lives. God never intended for our default style of ministry to become "drop-in service"—where we show up, do something helpful, and then go back to our real lives. Rather, we are to live incarnationally among those who are part of our real lives: coworkers, bosses, neighbors, teachers, friends, family. It's like going to a wedding—and we know Jesus attended weddings. We may not like everyone there. They may not be the people we would have chosen. But they are part of the fabric of our lives, and we are called to live incarnationally among them.

Robert Gelinas put it this way: "All too often we think it is our job to get people in a place where they can call on God, but what if God has already called them? Then our role in someone's life is to help them respond to the overtures of God." It's not just helping non-Christians cross a line into becoming Christians—it's "How can we come alongside what the Spirit's already trying to do in that person's life?"

Principle #3: Living with purpose

Jesus wasn't just wandering around Israel aimlessly. He was walking with a purpose. As we seek to live incarnationally, as he did, we too need to walk with a purpose. That doesn't mean we're in a hurry or that we're not relational—quite the contrary, actually. But it means that we view ourselves as being sent, and know that we are going about doing the work of the Father. As Jesus himself said, "In fact, the reason I was born and came into the world is to testify to the truth" (John 18:37).

Jesus had a clear sense of why he came into this world. We may not have that same clarity regarding our own unique purpose, but we figure it out as we go in the context of community. We can gain a clear picture of the overall missional journey, even as we recognize that our part lies somewhere within it.

Jesus was intentional about where he went and what he did, yet he was

How can you increase your intentionality and purpose? It's easy to get distracted by so many good things that we fail to focus on what's truly important. Intentional living requires consistent reflection and alignment with God's purpose for your life. What might it look like to develop a regular habit of reflection and alignment in your week?
- Dave

also sensitive to the Spirit when opportunities came up. He let his sense of purpose guide him, as he decided where to focus his attention and when to avoid distractions—and when those distractions should become his focus. Consider these passages:

> As the time approached for him to be taken up to heaven, Jesus resolutely set out for Jerusalem. And he sent messengers on ahead, who went into a Samaritan village to get things ready for him (Luke 9:51–52).

> When Jesus reached the spot, he looked up and said to him, "Zacchaeus, come down immediately. I must stay at your house today" (Luke 19:5).

> While Jesus was still talking to the crowd, his mother and brothers stood outside, wanting to speak to him. Someone told him, "Your mother and brothers are standing outside, wanting to speak to you." He replied to him, "Who is my mother, and who are my brothers?" Pointing to his disciples, he said, "Here are my mother and my brothers. For whoever does the will of my Father in heaven is my brother and sister and mother" (Matt. 12:46–50).

Principle #4: Engaging authentically with others

Jesus not only lived among the people and became part of the culture around him—he also interacted with people at a very personal level. He treated them as individuals, and engaged in conversations with them around issues that mattered to them. He talked with Nicodemus about his questions. He talked with the woman at the well about her needs. He expressed a wide range of emotions including anger, sadness, and love.

It's easy to consider people as interruptions in your day. With so much work to do, authentic conversations are often avoided, out of "necessity." What if you viewed your relationships as the work that God has given you to do? How might that change the way you engage with people?

- Dave

One of the interesting things about how Jesus engaged with others is that he treated each person differently; there was no formula. He met people where they were at, not where he thought they should be. He tested hearts for receptivity, and then gave each person what he or she needed. Consider the complexity of his interaction with the Canaanite woman:

Leaving that place, Jesus withdrew to the region of Tyre and Sidon. A Canaanite woman from that vicinity came to him, crying out, "Lord, Son of David, have mercy on me! My daughter is demon-possessed and suffering terribly."

Jesus did not answer a word. So his disciples came to him and urged him, "Send her away, for she keeps crying out after us." He answered, "I was sent only to the lost sheep of Israel." The woman came and knelt before him. "Lord, help me!" she said. He replied, "It is not right to take the children's bread and toss it to the dogs." "Yes it is, Lord," she said. "Even the dogs eat the crumbs that fall from their master's table."

Then Jesus said to her, "Woman, you have great faith! Your request is granted." And her daughter was healed at that moment (Matt. 15:21–28).

Authentic engagement is rare. So when it happens, people notice. Most people are rarely asked questions with any sort of depth. Most people are rarely listened to as they talk about the things that really matter to them. When we do these things, the doors of transformation and spiritual power are opened wide.

Principle #5: Serving the "least of these"

A principle that really seemed to jump from the pages of the gospels when I read through them is Jesus' focus on the least of these. That's where he really focused his ministry. Jesus was sent to proclaim good news to the poor, sight for the blind, and freedom for the oppressed (Luke 4:16–21). He was constantly hanging out with the poor, the disabled, the uneducated, cultural or ethnic minorities, women, and social outcasts. He talked about them and to them. He highlighted them, bringing them to the center of public attention.

When in the last month have you spent time with the poor, the disabled, the uneducated, or cultural or ethnic minorities? If you are going to "be Jesus," it's going to change who you hang out with. How might you develop a habit of serving the least, the last, and the lost?
- Dave

How many stories can you think of involving these people groups? The good Samaritan, the Samaritan woman at the well, the blind beggar, Lazarus at the gate, the woman caught in adultery, the healing of the Roman Centurion's son, the widow giving two coins, the lepers, the lame man trying to enter the healing waters, the gentile woman begging for crumbs from the table, the calling of tax collectors and fishermen as disciples. The list goes on and on and on.

> *"Then the King will say to those on his right, 'Come, you who are blessed by my Father; take your inheritance, the kingdom prepared for you since the creation of the world. For I was hungry and you gave me something to eat, I was thirsty and you gave me something to drink, I was a stranger and you invited me in, I needed clothes and you clothed me, I was sick and you looked after me, I was in prison and you came to visit me.'*

> *"Then the righteous will answer him, 'Lord, when did we see you hungry and feed you, or thirsty and give you something to drink? When did we see you a stranger and invite you in, or needing clothes and clothe you? When did we see you sick or in prison and go to visit you?'*

> *"The King will reply, 'Truly I tell you, whatever you did for one of the least of these brothers and sisters of mine, you did for me'" (Matt. 25: 34–40).*

Based on my reading of scripture, I've concluded that if we're not engaged in serving the "least of these," we're not connecting to the heart of God.

We know who the "least of these" were during Jesus' time on earth: Lepers, women, uneducated fishermen, the diseased, the blind, prostitutes, tax collectors, the racial-minority Samaritans, and those who had to stay outside the temple walls because they were unclean. These are the people Jesus went to, and these were the people who were most receptive to him.

Who are the "least of these" today? They are AIDS victims, illegal immigrants, gays, homeless people, ethnic minorities, Muslims, runaway teens, people on welfare, the mentally ill, addicts, prisoners, profiteering business people, sex offenders who must live outside the city limits, and prostitutes (that last category hasn't changed at all in 2,000 years). Jesus wasn't afraid to touch anyone. How willing are we, the church, to follow in his footsteps? Or are we more afraid, as the Pharisees were, of "contaminating" ourselves?

Principle #6: Calling people to follow Jesus

This principle reflects Jesus' final command to us that we make disciples, "teaching them to obey everything I've commanded you."

Jesus didn't shy away from calling people toward commitment, but he approached it in a surprisingly wide variety of ways. He was gracious to those who were struggling. He was unrelenting to those whose hearts were hard. What determined his response? Although we can't be

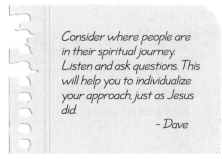

Consider where people are in their spiritual journey. Listen and ask questions. This will help you to individualize your approach, just as Jesus did.

- Dave

certain, he seemed to individualize his approach based on several different factors: who each person was, the condition of their hearts, their motives for talking with Jesus, what it was they really needed to know, and what direction their lives were currently moving in.

Jesus was full of both grace and truth: accepting of where people were, yet encouraging them to go the next step. Understanding and grace-filled, yet capable of strong challenge when it was called for. He didn't do just one or the other, but both. And he did ask for a response.

> Then he called the crowd to him along with his disciples and said: "Whoever wants to be my disciple must deny themselves and take up their cross and follow me. For whoever wants to save their life will lose it, but whoever loses their life for me and for the gospel will save it. What good is it for someone to gain the whole world, yet forfeit their soul? Or what can anyone give in exchange for their soul?"(Mark 8:34–37).

Jesus never forced anyone to respond, but he did present people with choices about coming into relationship with him. I'm assuming we should follow suit, listening to the Holy Spirit and using our discernment as we consider the best approach for each person God places in our lives.

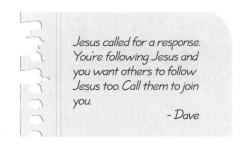

Jesus called for a response. You're following Jesus and you want others to follow Jesus too. Call them to join you.

- Dave

Principle #7: Cultivating others to live incarnationally

Leave it to Jesus to be forward-looking. He knew the time would come when he couldn't be there with his followers, and thus he showed them how to do things. He taught them how to figure out the next steps. He shaped their characters and prepared them to learn to listen to the Holy Spirit who would come. He encouraged them to engage in service and learn as they go.

The very last thing he told us was to make more disciples. We are specifically charged with cultivating others to live incarnationally as followers of Jesus. In fact, that's part of following him—cultivating others to live and love like Jesus did.

Like Jesus, we need to prepare our people to serve and to lead when we are no longer there to guide them. We may choose unlikely candidates (as Jesus certainly did), but we can invest in them relationally, engage them in an apprenticing process, and help them serve with an eye toward multiplying themselves as well.

> I'm convinced that every Christian needs to follow Jesus and help others to follow Jesus.
>
> First step: Follow Jesus by living out these seven principles.
>
> Second step: Help others to follow Jesus by living out these seven principles.
> - With whom will you start?
> - How could your team support one another in living out these principles?
>
> — Dave

After this the Lord appointed seventy-two others and sent them two by two ahead of him to every town and place where he was about to go. He told them, "The harvest is plentiful, but the workers are few. Ask the Lord of the harvest, therefore, to send out workers into his harvest field. Go! I am sending you out like lambs among wolves (Luke 10:1–3).

Jesus expected that his own disciples would do as he did, and that included raising up disciples. He taught, "The student is not above the teacher, but everyone who is fully trained will be like their teacher" (Luke 6:40). Jesus made apprentices, taught them to do as he did, and lived among them. If we are his disciples, we are to do the same as we cultivate others.

These seven principles are what Jesus meant when he said to make disciples of all nations. Living as Jesus lived is inextricably linked to doing what Jesus told us to do.

What did Jesus tell us to do?

As we increasingly learn to live as Jesus lived, following his example, the result is that we do what Jesus told us to do. We obey not out of fear, but out of love and a shared vision for the good news of the Kingdom of God.

So what did Jesus tell us to do? Any glance at a red-letter version of the Bible shows that he said quite a lot—and that some of the things he said make more sense to our contemporary ears than others. How do we sift through all the teachings of Jesus and interpret them?

For our purposes here, I'd suggest a general-principle approach. In other words, we take the broadest general teachings that encompass all the rest of what Jesus said. You're certainly welcome to select your own red-letter passages, but I'd suggest these two:

The great commandment: Matt. 22:34–40
Hearing that Jesus had silenced the Sadducees, the Pharisees got together. One of them, an expert in the law, tested him with this question: "Teacher, which is the greatest commandment in the Law?"

Jesus replied: "'Love the Lord your God with all your heart and with all your soul and with all your mind. This is the first and greatest commandment. And the second is like it: 'Love your neighbor as yourself.' All the Law and the Prophets hang on these two commandments."

The great commission: Matt. 28:18–20
Then Jesus came to them and said, "All authority in heaven and on earth has been given to me. Therefore go and make disciples of all nations, baptizing them in the name of the Father and of the Son and of the Holy Spirit, and teaching them to obey everything I have commanded you. And surely I am with you always, to the very end of the age."

The great commandment was said by Jesus to sum up all the law and the prophets. It also encompasses many of Jesus' other teachings on how we are to relate to God and others. The great commission is probably the most direct case of Jesus asking us to do something, and it also represents his last words to us on earth. Because it is clearly geared toward the mission he left for his future generations of disciples.

I would make the case that all of Jesus other teachings can be fit under the major headings of the great commandment and the great commission: love God, love others, make disciples. If we can keep these teachings of Jesus in the forefront of our minds, we'll stay on the right course.

Wow! Did you catch that statement? "It's very difficult to live incarnationally and not make disciples." Yet there are so many people who claim to be following Jesus, but who have never personally made disciples. The key is to start living incarnationally. You'll discover that disciplemaking happens more naturally when you do.

– Dave

As we live like Jesus lived and do what he told us to do, we will see the fruit of that. We'll see people in authentic relationships, serving others sacrificially, and being transformed by the power of God. We'll see disciples made, communities of Jesus followers growing, and neighborhoods transformed. In fact, it's very difficult to live incarnationally and not make disciples. People will be curious. They'll be impacted. They'll want to know why you're doing the things you're doing. And at least some of them will want to get in on it.

So as we live incarnationally, we look for those who are responsive and help them as they are ready. This is what Jesus meant when he said to make disciples: Do what I have done with you to others from all nations.

How can we live this out, with all of our imperfections?

All of this may feel a little overwhelming: Live as Jesus lived. Do what Jesus taught. It's like the first time I read through a gospel account and quickly came across Matthew 5:48: *"Be perfect, therefore, as your heavenly Father is perfect."* I might as well shut the book right there, I thought, given the chances I have of living up to that standard.

There's no way we're going to be perfect. But if we're simply moving in the right direction, stumbling forward as best we can, we'll see the Spirit at work and catch glimpses of the Kingdom. Even with all of our imperfections, we do have contributions to make. That's how Jesus intended it to be:

"Very truly I tell you, whoever believes in me will do the works I have been doing, and they will do even greater things than these, because I am going to the Father" (John 14:12).

Each one of us has something to contribute. It doesn't matter what our age, our income, our situation in life, our past failures, our limitations are. As Theodore Roosevelt said: "Do what you can, with what you have, where you are." God gave each of us spiritual gifts to be used for the benefit of others and for the extending of the Kingdom. He also gave us the Holy Spirit, to help us discern how to move forward into what God has for us. We all have something to contribute.

One of the biggest blockages to living as Jesus lived is our sense that we should be doing something huge, something amazing, something on a large scale. And if we think that way, of course we'll never do anything at all. It's too overwhelming. Instead, we need to think "baby steps." We don't have to do everything… but we do have to do something. So find something to do. Start small. See how it goes. You can always add from there later. But get started now.

> When I was a child, my mom used to say to me, "Do it now. Do it now. Do it now." She knew that I had a tendency to procrastinate and put things off. As Christians, we can often put off getting started until later. Don't do that! What's one thing you can do today to get started? Do it now!
> - Dave

We all have something to contribute. It doesn't have to be huge. But when all the little pieces come together, it makes something huge. Bishop Desmond Tutu said: "Do your little bit of good where you are; it's those little bits of good put together that overwhelm the world." Together, many small things can add up to real change. It's like that with the body of Christ. When we all do our "little bit of good," it comes together to create something greater than the sum of the parts. All these little things together change the world.

That's what we're talking about with the good news of the Kingdom of God—all of these small acts from all of these different people coming together to contribute to the larger vision of the Kingdom of God, "on earth as it is in heaven" (Matt. 6:10).

So what is your "little bit of good"? Find out, and do it with all your might.

Journey Guide: Incarnational ministry

Discussion questions: for you and your team

- What does incarnational ministry look like?
- How did Jesus live?
- What did Jesus tell us to do?
- How can we live that out, with all of our imperfections?
- What is your little bit of good?

Guided prayer: for you and your team

Pray through each of the seven principles of incarnational living, together with your team. Plan to spend a few minutes in reflection on each principle and introduce each one with "How can we...."

- ...stay connected with the Father?
- ...integrate into the culture?
- ...live with purpose?
- ...engage authentically with others?
- ...serve the "least of these"?
- ...call people to follow Jesus?
- ...cultivate others to live incarnationally?

Planning questions: for you and your coach

- How are you living as Jesus lived?
- What is working well?
- What needs to change?
- If your team members were to carefully observe how you live, what principles of incarnational living would they draw from your actions?
- How are you helping others to live incarnationally?

To do list: action points to implement

- _____

- _____

- _____

Chapter 3

What does it mean to be the church?

The word *church*, to most people today, brings to mind an institution. Yet the church was never intended to be an institution; it was intended to be a movement of people living incarnationally together.

As Jesus' disciples increasingly learned to live as Jesus lived, and do what Jesus told them to do, the result was that they made more disciples. These disciples then naturally gathered together into what we now call churches. The biblical word for church is "ecclesia," which simply means gathering or assembly. Do you see the progression?

incarnational living ⟶ disciples ⟶ churches

The basic DNA of the church is found in the gospels. Disciples carry this DNA. Disciples, when gathered together, are called churches. Churches are actually a by-product—a result of a way of living. They are organic, not institutional.

Words have meaning. Take some time to reflect on the meaning of each of these words. Write out your "personal shorthand" meaning for each of these terms.
- Dave

For what it's worth, here's my personal shorthand for all of these terms:

Kingdom: The reign of God on earth as it is in heaven; a reality that reflects the heart of God. The Kingdom of God is lived out through sacrificial service, authentic relationships, and spiritual transformation.

Disciple: One who is intentionally following Jesus, becoming like Jesus, and living like Jesus in community with others on mission.

Gospel: The story of Jesus' life, death, and resurrection, reflected by transformed lives that express the Kingdom of God on earth.

Church: The gathering of believers who together live out the Kingdom, communicate the gospel, and make disciples.

Missional: Any person or group of people who are focused on living in accordance with the great commandment and the great commission.

When the church was birthed in Acts, it was a matter of the disciples figuring out how to express that DNA corporately. How would they live it out together? The story flows from the end of the gospel accounts through the beginning of Acts. The last words of Jesus in the gospels were his command to make disciples:

> *Then Jesus came to them and said, "All authority in heaven and on earth has been given to me. Therefore go and make disciples of all nations, baptizing them in the name of the Father and of the Son and of the Holy Spirit, and teaching them to obey everything I have commanded you. And surely I am with you always, to the very end of the age" (Matt. 28:18–20).*

Then we move into Acts 1:

> *On one occasion, while he was eating with them, he gave them this command: "Do not leave Jerusalem, but wait for the gift my Father promised, which you have heard me speak about. For John baptized with water, but in a few days you will be baptized with the Holy Spirit."*

> *Then they gathered around him and asked him, "Lord, are you at this time going to restore the kingdom to Israel?"*

> *He said to them: "It is not for you to know the times or dates the Father has set by his own authority. But you will receive power when the Holy Spirit comes on you; and you will be my witnesses in Jerusalem, and in all Judea and Samaria, and to the ends of the earth" (Acts 1:4–8).*

We see that the twelve were unable to make disciples on their own. They needed the power of the Holy Spirit. Jesus knew this—and told them to stay in Jerusalem waiting and praying. It was only after the coming of the Spirit at Pentecost in Acts 2 that we see the formation of the church and the beginning of the fulfillment of the great commission. Let's look at the church that emerges:

Those who accepted his message were baptized, and about three thousand were added to their number that day.

> *They devoted themselves to the apostles' teaching and to fellowship, to the breaking of bread and to prayer. Everyone was filled with awe at the many wonders and signs performed by the apostles. All the believers were together and had everything in common. They sold property and possessions to give to anyone who had need. Every day they continued to meet together in the temple courts. They broke bread in their homes and ate together with glad and sincere hearts, praising God and enjoying the favor of all the people. And the Lord added to their number daily those who were being saved (Acts 2:41–47).*

And this is just one passage. We have the whole rest of Acts and the Epistles to see what the church did. Below is an incomplete listing of some of the functions of the church found in scripture:

- They confessed sins.
- They celebrated the Lord's supper.
- They baptized.
- The both gathered and scattered.
- They reached out and engaged the culture around them.
- They continued to carry out the apostolic ministry of Jesus, doing the works he did.
- They engaged in ministry to the poor and hurting.
- They focused on equipping.
- Everyone had a role to play; everyone had spiritual gifts to use.
- They had a leadership structure.
- They commissioned and sent out missionaries.
- When problems arose, they consulted others.
- The churches in different locations were connected in the same movement.

What else does the church do? List as many additional functions of the church as you can.

- Dave

During the first century, the church was in a challenging season of figuring out what it meant to be the church—and as we seek to discover today what it means to be the church, we can learn a lot from them. As the earliest disciples gathered, what qualities of their life together allowed them to make more disciples? How did they express the DNA of Jesus found in the gospels? How did they translate Jesus' behavior into various contexts and cultures? What behaviors do we see in Acts and the epistles?

What is the church supposed to do?

We are the church! Understanding what the church is actually supposed to be doing helps us as individual Christians understand what we're supposed to be doing. It also helps us to understand the disciple-making process better, as we join together in helping new followers of Christ to do these same things.

- Dave

It's a practical question: What are we, as the church, actually supposed to be doing? What is our purpose? What are the actions that would demonstrate that purpose? Although there are many, many possible answers to this question, almost all of them would fall generally under one of the following three categories:

• Sacrificial service
• Authentic relationships
• Spiritual transformation

These are the core ingredients of the missional journey. They represent what it means to be a follower of Jesus. Together, they bring about broader societal transformation in line with the Kingdom of God.

Sacrificial service

When Jesus washed his disciples' feet he said, "*Now that I, your Lord and Teacher, have washed your feet, you also should wash one another's feet. I have set you an example that you should do as I have done for you. Very truly I tell you, no servant is greater than his master, nor is a messenger greater than the one who sent him. Now that you know these things, you will be blessed if you do them*" (John 13:14–17). We are to follow Jesus' example in providing humble, sacrificial service to others.

Just as Jesus served the poor, healed the sick, and brought hope to the broken, we are to follow in his footsteps. We are sent on mission to the world around us. We were not only meant to love and serve one another within the body of Christ, but everyone. After all, the question "Who is my neighbor?" was answered with the parable of the Good Samaritan (see Luke 10:25–37). We are to serve those around us with our gifts, our time, and our money.

> When we view church as something we do on Sunday mornings, we can easily view our "ministry" as serving other Christians. Yet, when we understand that church is who we are, it opens up opportunities to serve beyond the walls of the church as well. Both are essential.
>
> – Dave

That means all people, but especially the "least of these." When Paul and Barnabas were sent forth on mission to serve, the other apostles had only one injunction: *"All they asked was that we should continue to remember the poor, the very thing I had been eager to do all along"* (Gal. 2:10). Being mindful and generous in the face of poverty was that important to the church. The church that represents the coming of the Kingdom of God engages in sacrificial service to the world around us. And it never forgets the poor.

Austin New Church in Austin, Texas cancels their Sunday gatherings on a regular basis to engage in what they call "Serve Austin." Their people can be involved in fifteen different mission sites around the city that serve in various ways: serving food, painting classrooms, cleaning parks, etc. These Sundays have consistently higher participation than "regular" Sundays. Austin New Church is also becoming well known in the community for not offering an Easter service each year, but instead practicing "pure religion" based on James 1: serving hamburgers and communion to the homeless.

The Winnipeg Vineyard Church in Winnipeg, Manitoba had been raising funds to buy a building, but instead felt God calling them to give all the money they'd raised to a church plant in Kathmandu, Nepal. The ministry they gave the money to works among the poorest of the poor, who live along the banks of the river that flows through the city. In this river, the people wash, drink, and dispose of the ashes of the dead.

LifeHouse Christian Church in Vancouver, British Columbia is a network of organic house churches that ministers to sex offenders. Society at large rejects these modern-day lepers, considering them impossible to rehabilitate and chasing them out of their communities. Yet this church, in conjunction with a Mennonite nonprofit group, asks how they might walk with them in the path of redemption wisely, without endangering anyone. They provide them with accountability, a faith community, and emotional support for the long difficult journey of change ahead of them.

There are many, many different ways we can provide sacrificial service to the "least of these."

Authentic relationships

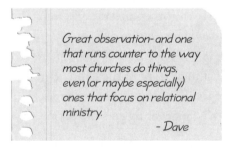

Great observation- and one that runs counter to the way most churches do things, even (or maybe especially) ones that focus on relational ministry.

- Dave

Often we look for authentic relationships with other believers before engaging in sacrificial service with them. That approach is seldom successful, since it's based on our own needs and desires rather than a willingness to give and pour out of our lives into the lives of others. But if we turn it around—if we engage in sacrificial service alongside other believers—it's almost impossible to avoid authentic relationships. They just happen.

What kind of authentic relationships are we talking about? The relationships that result from living out the "one-another" commandments within the body of Christ:

- Be devoted to one another in love.
- Honor one another above yourselves.
- Live in harmony with one another.
- Serve one another humbly in love.
- Be kind and compassionate to one another.
- Forgive one another.
- Teach and admonish one another.
- Encourage one another.
- Love one another as brothers and sisters.

It's in the context of community and relationship that we disciple one another, sharpen one another, and equip one another for good deeds and service. This is where discipleship happens. Discipleship isn't just done in groups, and it isn't just done one-on-one—it's both. Everyone has their own journey, but that journey must take place in the context of missional community.

What would happen if a person was only discipled one-on-one and never experienced the benefits of community in a small group? Conversely, what would happen if discipleship only happened in groups, without any personal guidance or input? Making disciples happens best through individual and group interaction.

- Dave

Authentic relationships aren't just limited to other believers. We're called to engage honestly and respectfully with those who see life differently than we do. We are to take the initiative to be present and hospitable. We are to be our authentic selves—sharing our joys, struggles, doubts, and beliefs—as we engage in relationships.

Adullam Church in Denver, Colorado lives out a 2-1-1 rhythm in all their missional community groups—meaning: they gather four times a month, with two gatherings focused on relationship with God, one gathering focused on mission and serving, and one gathering that's simply a party. They invite friends

Discipleship flows out of relationship. Consider the people with whom you have relationship. Who could you have a meaningful conversation with, about how you're learning to follow Jesus?

- Dave

and acquaintances into homes instead of churches and do normal, relational things together. One of the more popular parties has been guys' poker night. Because people just keep inviting other people, at this point they have twenty guys attending—about half believers, half not—with everyone having a chance to host if they want to. When there's a natural social network established, it's easier to engage in authentic relationships.

Authentic relationships produce trust and relational equity. An Australian business coach invited a number of his associates to come to his house on a Sunday afternoon for a wine, cheese, and coffee gathering to talk about spirituality. Virtually everyone he invited came because of their relationship with him. They had worked with him for years, knew he was a follower of Jesus, and trusted him. As a part of that process, they got into some meaningful conversations and a number of the people decided to become followers of Jesus.

Spiritual transformation

As we serve sacrificially and engage in authentic relationships, something else begins to happen: transformation. By engaging with others, we have also engaged with God: *"The King will reply, 'Truly I tell you, whatever you did for one of the least of these brothers and sisters of mine, you did for me'"* (Matt. 25:40). We experience transformation as we interact with God, with each other, and as we serve. We see the power of the gospel transforming us, others, and the communities around us.

We're talking about the confession of sin and the expression of grace— repentance, changed lives, baptism, and the celebration of the Lord's supper. We cannot truly engage with God without coming away changed, like Moses when he met God face to face.

How's your prayer habit? How are you persisting in prayer? I love the PUSH approach to prayer - Pray Until Something Happens. Don't just pray once - persevere in prayer. Then see how your prayer infuses your relationships.

- Dave

When Moses came down from Mount Sinai with the two tablets of the covenant law in his hands, he was not aware that his face was radiant because he had spoken with the LORD. When Aaron and all the Israelites saw Moses, his face was radiant, and they were afraid to come near him. But Moses called to them; so Aaron and all the leaders of the community came back to him, and he spoke to them. Afterward all the Israelites came near him, and he gave them all the commands the LORD had given him on Mount Sinai (Exodus 34:29–32).

We see the early church experiencing the kind of worship that comes from a transformed life. Prayer infused the life of the early church. They prayed for strength, courage, and the power of the Holy Spirit. They prayed in the name of Jesus. They prayed to connect with the Father. They prayed for and with one another. They prayed for more workers for the harvest fields. They prayed through spiritual warfare. They prayed for the coming of the Kingdom of God, and worshiped God together… and their transformation resulted in a transformed community around them.

Austin Stone Community Church took the money they had set aside for a new building and purchased land in the highest crime rate area in Austin. On that land they built a community mission center to serve the city around them. For their worship services, they began setting up and tearing down every week in a school gymnasium. They invested *outside* their church rather than inside—and that year their church doubled in size.

The gospel has even greatly impacted the social fabric of a village high up in the Himalayas. As a result of a new church plant there, the way people in the village treat women has changed dramatically. Women are now respected rather than beaten, and they hold leadership positions in the church. Another significant impact has been financial. In the past the people had spent a significant portion of income on purchasing amulets from Buddhist monks to protect them from demonic forces. Now Jesus gives them, without cost, what they used to pay for.

A missional church of about 140 people in Australia had been meeting in a school hall. Although they had rented the space, they asked the principal how they could best serve the school. No one had ever asked that question before, so the principal was a bit taken aback. Nonetheless, as a relationship developed the church began to pick up on different needs the school had: jumpers (sweaters) for migrant students in winter who could not afford them, lunch packs for students whose families were going through tough times, church-sponsored awards for student achievement (given anonymously—

not with the church's name all over them). People from the church also sometimes brought in coffee for the school staff, or held teacher-appreciation events.

One day the principal expressed the desire to have a complete makeover for the school grounds. The pastor picked up on that thought and mobilized the church for action, even though they had no budget for a project of that scope. They called this project "Day of Difference" (although it ended up being more like six weeks of difference). The vision was shared, the landscaping plan was made, and through this small missional church, all kinds of different organizations pitched in: community organizations, local tradespeople, local service groups, and a combination volunteers from both churches and the community rallied together for this day of difference. More than $40,000 was raised to contribute to the school makeover, and an estimated $80,000 was donated in kind through free skills, labor, equipment, service, and material.

On the official "Day of Difference," more than three hundred volunteers came together and spent the day completely reshaping and renewing this local school. Painting, planting, building gardens, and creating new recreational spaces transformed the campus. A city radio station did a live broadcast from the school about the project, and an interstate truck driver heard about it over the radio. After unloading his freight, he drove his rig to the school and helped for three hours, building the gardens.

The church is now regularly involved with the PTA parent group, it sponsors a full-time chaplain within the school, and the relationship continues to strengthen. The opportunity to live like Jesus lived is increasing and resulting in changed lives.

The tension

There is an inherent tension at the place where these three tasks of the church—sacrificial service, authentic relationships, and spiritual transformation—intersect. How are these three tasks related to one another, and when are they affected by misguided motives? Are we serving sacrificially simply to get people to engage in spiritual transformation (e.g., you can have the soup if you listen to the sermon)? Are we engaging in authentic relationships to move them toward spiritual transformation (e.g., I'm trying to be your friend so I can invite you to church)? In both of those cases, the adjective would need to be removed. That kind of serving is no longer sacrificial, but self-interested. Likewise, those kinds of relationships certainly could not be called authentic.

Do you feel the tension? When I worked with the original core team for my most recent church plant, we certainly did. A team member raised a concern: He wanted to serve others without any hidden agenda, giving freely rather than giving in order to try to get people to make a faith commitment. His point was valid. We decided that we would serve as Jesus served. Whether people were responsive to the gospel or not, we would serve them anyway, with no agenda.

> Some people think, "I witness with my actions." Others think, "I witness with my words." Both are necessary. We need to demonstrate the gospel and articulate the gospel. As you serve sacrificially, look for responsive people with whom you can share the story of Jesus.
>
> - Dave

At the same time, we committed ourselves to Jesus' command to make disciples. As we serve, we expect that some will encounter God through our actions. We are committed to actively keeping our eyes and ears attuned for those who are spiritually open. And we continue to engage in spiritual dialogue, sharing the gospel and encouraging others to become followers of Jesus.

We are doing both—not serving so we can make disciples, but serving and making disciples. That's an important distinction. It's easy for people to go one way or the other, but we need both. Dividing the temporal from the spiritual is an artificial forced choice. Worse than that, either one without the other doesn't work—each one alone invalidates itself—cheating people out of the richness and fullness of the Kingdom.

If we get so focused on the spiritual that we ignore temporal needs, we're not living like Jesus did; and if so, no wonder people are critical. On the other hand, we can't forget the very last thing Jesus told us to do: make disciples

(Matt. 28:19-20). So we must help people deal with their eternal state, and be people who are fully like Jesus in the moment, living as Jesus did.

> *Very truly I tell you, whoever believes in me will do the works I have been doing, and they will do even greater things than these, because I am going to the Father (John 14:12).*

What about us?

We are the continuation of the early church that we read about in scripture. Our own missional community descends from the believers in the book of Acts. How will we express the transforming power of the Holy Spirit today? What actions will we take? How we address questions like this determines how we will be the church today.

Our values need to be linked to our behaviors or they aren't really values—they are just preferences. If it's truly a value, it will be expressed in action. How are your values seen in your actions? How can these practices become habits of your community?

Use the chart to help you think through your values and the actions that reflect those values.

What values do you want your church to express?	What are some concrete actions that could express those values?

Organizing for ministry

All life requires organization to sustain itself; without structure life can't happen. Certainly, we can over-structure and kill life, such as when a church becomes just an institution. But some structure is not only valuable, but essential for life. Even the simplest living thing requires organization of some kind. The church—being alive—is no different. A logical function of any gathering is that some organization is needed, otherwise it's just a crowd with no purpose.

> Some groups find it helpful to define their values first, then clarify behaviors that flow from those values. It may also be helpful to list the behaviors you're already practicing, and then identify the values that drive these behaviors. You could also try reading Acts 2:42-47 and listing the behaviors of the early church, and then identifying the values behind those behaviors. You can do this exercise in either order—it's not linear but part of a back-and-forth cycle.
> -Dave

How did the early church organize its ministry? In the early chapters of Acts, we see the former disciples becoming apostles and functioning in leadership roles. They interacted with the people, healed sickness, and taught the good news of Jesus. They responded to persecution with faith and confidence. They essentially served as models for other believers to follow.

Then in Acts 6, the church grew to the point that a new level was added to the leadership structure:

> In those days when the number of disciples was increasing, the Hellenistic Jews among them complained against the Hebraic Jews because their widows were being overlooked in the daily distribution of food. So the Twelve gathered all the disciples together and said, "It would not be right for us to neglect the ministry of the word of God in order to wait on tables. Brothers and sisters,

> A church planter once told me, "We don't need structure or leadership; we are organic." This led to a great discussion on the reality that everything organic has some kind of structure. Don't fall into the trap of thinking that structure is unnecessary. Instead, focus on keeping structure simple and functional.
> - Dave

choose seven men from among you who are known to be full of the Spirit and wisdom. We will turn this responsibility over to them and will give our attention to prayer and the ministry of the word."

This proposal pleased the whole group. They chose Stephen, a man full of faith and of the Holy Spirit; also Philip, Procorus, Nicanor, Timon, Parmenas, and Nicolas from Antioch, a convert to Judaism. They presented these men to the apostles, who prayed and laid their hands on them.

So the word of God spread. The number of disciples in Jerusalem increased rapidly, and a large number of priests became obedient to the faith (Acts 6:1–7).

We still see this kind of shift in churches today. In very small gatherings, a handful of leaders can shepherd the people, but as the needs and the demands on leaders' time increase, more leaders must share the workload. If churches are unwilling to empower more leaders, growth stops and the church begins receding.

Raising leaders from the harvest is vital. Don't wait for God to send you leaders. Don't focus on recruiting leaders from outside. Focus on raising up leaders from within. Begin to consider how you'll mentor and coach new leaders.

- Dave

Not only is the distribution of various responsibilities necessary to get all the work done, but it's also an essential ingredient for growing individuals within the church and teaching them to use their God-given spiritual gifts. Consider the following excerpts from 1 Corinthians 12:

There are different kinds of gifts, but the same Spirit distributes them…. Now to each one the manifestation of the Spirit is given for the common good. To one there is given through the Spirit a message of wisdom, to another a message of knowledge by means of the same Spirit, to another faith by the same Spirit, to another gifts of healing by that one Spirit….Just as a body, though one, has many parts, but all its many parts form one body, so it is with Christ….

Now if the foot should say, "Because I am not a hand, I do not belong to the body," it would not for that reason stop being part of the body. And if the ear should say, "Because I am not an eye, I do not belong to the body," it would not for that reason stop being part of the body. If the whole body were an eye, where would the sense of hearing be? If the whole body were an ear, where would the sense of smell be? But in fact God has placed the parts in the body, every one of them, just as he wanted them to be....Now you are the body of Christ, and each one of you is a part of it (1 Cor. 12:4, 7–9, 12, 15–18, 27).

The body of Christ—the church—is organic, living, and growing. Yet that doesn't mean it lacks structure. On the contrary, the body of Christ is structured flexibly to be able to adapt and respond more effectively to its surroundings. God has given us the gifts we need to be able to do that.

Model of ministry

There are an almost infinite number of ways to structure a church, and there's no one way that's right for everyone. It's a matter of choosing a structure that will help grow and sustain life rather than killing it. If we're engaging culture and forming communities, we'll need some way to organize those communities and support the leaders. So how do we choose?

I believe in focusing on underlying principles, rather than prescribing specific models. Models change—principles don't. In fact I should probably put our cards on the table right now. Let me state my biases up front: I've planted a classic model of church; I've planted a network of missional house churches with multi-ethnic leaders; and I've started non-church ministry organizations. As a coach and consultant I have experience working with a variety of models, and I'm not here to tell you

Just a word of caution about copying another's model for ministry. Many church planters and pastors become enamored with a certain model of ministry and try to replicate it.

Unfortunately, church methodology sells. Across the country, successful churches are helping unsuccessful churches to copy their strategies, methods, programs, and worship services. It can become very easy to simply substitute what works for someone else somewhere else in place of really hearing the voice of the Spirit and following his leadership for your ministry in your current context. God does not want clones. If he did, he would have given more specific instructions in the Bible about how to do church.
– Dave

which model to use. As long as the focus is missional and the people are living incarnationally, it doesn't matter what kind of model or structure we use. It takes all kinds of ministries to build the Kingdom.

The smallest unit of ministry is usually a gathering of five to twelve. Some ministries call these groups churches—as in the house-church model. Other people call those gatherings cells or groups, and only a larger gathering is called a church. Still other ministries call those groups missional communities and eschew the word "church" altogether.

At a grassroots level, these small communities—no matter what you call them—function similarly. How these communities network together with one another and how often they gather depends on the model being followed. Some ministries never gather their smaller communities together. Others gather quarterly, monthly, weekly, or even daily (see Acts 2:46). The point is, how we decide to frame the way in which our smallest units are connected to one another, and how they gather, becomes our model for ministry.

You may not have a strong preference of one model over another. But if you expect to get any work at all done, you'll have to come up with some kind of organizing principle—even if it's a very simple one. What will the organizing principle be for your ministry? How will you organize the disciples you make?

Obviously, this structure could look a lot of different ways. Let's run through some scenarios, to help you to start thinking it through:

- A decentralized network of house churches that maintain some type of tie with each other but do not share a common gathering
- Several missional communities that serve and make disciples, then gather together monthly for worship
- A large church, with many life groups that meet throughout the week
- A network of house-church groups that are banded together as one church and worship together periodically (quarterly or monthly)
- A mid-sized missional community led by lay leaders and including smaller huddles for more intensive discipleship.
- A network of leaders who meet together to learn how to better support their individual missional communities

There are many more options and shades in between, but you get the idea. Here are a few questions to help you further think through what type of organizing principle might work best for you:

- Where does worship take place?
- What unit will you measure to track growth?
- Which people are networked together?
- Where does the authority reside?
- How often do the different units come together?
- In what ways will the leaders network together, and how often?
- How will you develop new leaders?
- What unit are you trying to multiply?

How you answer these questions will give you some important clues as to how you'll want to structure your ministry. Remember: The structure you choose will contribute to the type of DNA you build. You need to mold our model to fit with your DNA, not vice versa. If you want service and discipleship to be your core activities, then you'll need to form your groups accordingly. Not all groups need to be Bible studies. Think creatively. Structure your groups to focus on your most central DNA, and then make them reproducible.

The goal of the church

As disciples were made, the church formed to become a gathering place for those disciples. The church, in turn, took on the mission Jesus left it—to make disciples. The church is to be a place of both gathering and outreach—a place for our own culture and a place for the reaching of other cultures.

Just like the early church was committed to making disciples, the church today must be committed to making disciples. Unfortunately, many churches today have lost any sense of mission, beyond serving the needs of its membership. How will you seize Jesus' mission as your own?

- Dave

Disciples gathered together in the church, lived out the Kingdom of God in community with other disciples on mission, and made more disciples. In doing so, the church grew. It grew by cooperating with the Holy Spirit and by structuring for maximum effectiveness. It grew through its goal of making disciples. It grew and multiplied from Jerusalem, to Judea and Samaria, to the ends of the earth.

We are the continuation of the early church that we read about in scripture. Our mission is the same today: to make disciples. The core ingredients of our missional journey are the same today: sacrificial service, authentic relationship, and spiritual transformation. The decisions we make about how we live that out will determine how we'll be the church in the world today.

Journey guide: The church

Discussion questions: for you and your team

- Consider some of the passages from Acts in this chapter. How would you compare some of those functions to what currently happens within your church plant?
- A missional community can serve all the basic functions of church. What elements would you like to see your missional communities include?
- Think specifically of your ministry team. What are some of the gifts the Holy Spirit has given?
- How would you go about determining the needs of your community?
- How might you address some of those needs, both within your church plant and in the surrounding community?

Guided prayer: for you and your team

Spend some time in prayer together with your team or group, asking God what he wants you—as the church—to do. What are you hearing? Write down thoughts on a whiteboard and consider how to respond.

Planning questions: for you and your coach

- How will your team engage in sacrificial service?
- How will your team engage in authentic relationships?
- How will your team engage in spiritual transformation?
- How will you engage in these three activities in a way that they don't conflict with one another?
- Draw a diagram that overviews the ministry flow in your church.

To do list: action points to implement

- _____
- _____
- _____
- _____

Chapter 4

How do we get there from here?

So far we've considered the Kingdom of God, what incarnational ministry looks like, and what it means to be the church. Taken together, those three concepts give us a sense of where we're trying to go—and of who we, as the people of God, are trying to be. The question now is how. How do we get there from here? How do we live out the kingdom in a way that replicates across cultures, languages and nations? How do we get from here…

For although they knew God, they neither glorified him as God nor gave thanks to him, but their thinking became futile and their foolish hearts were darkened. Although they claimed to be wise, they became fools and exchanged the glory of the immortal God for images made to look like a mortal human being and birds and animals and reptiles (Rom. 1:21–23).

…to here?

After this I looked, and there before me was a great multitude that no one could count, from every nation, tribe, people and language, standing before the throne and before the Lamb. They were wearing white robes and were holding palm branches in their hands. And they cried out in a loud voice: "Salvation belongs to our God, who sits on the throne, and to the Lamb" (Rev. 7:9–10).

Any endeavor of this scope must be rooted and built up in prayer. You and your team will need to be engaging God in prayer throughout the entire process. Action steps are good and necessary. But between each action step, your team needs to take the time to discern God's voice and clarify where he's leading.

The journey

A metaphor I've often used to describe the process of getting "from here to there"—accomplishing a goal—is that of a journey. I first introduced this metaphor in *From Followers to Leaders*; it can be explored in more depth in that book, but I'll tell the basic story here:

Every journey implies a destination. There is a goal and there is a process for getting there. Say we want to hike up a mountain. The destination is the view at the top of the mountain—that's the goal. Our starting point is quite different though. We start in the parking lot at the bottom of the mountain, asking ourselves, "Is it worth it?" Climbing the mountain will take time and effort and energy, so we need to consider if this journey is worth it to us.

If we decide that it is, we get out of the car and walk over to the trailhead. There we see a map to help us get oriented. It doesn't have all of the details, but it gives us a general idea of what to expect. At the trailhead we also meet the guide who will be leading a group out onto the trail. If after looking at the map and talking with the guide, we still think making the journey will be worth the effort, we move out onto the trail.

Where are you going? You have to know where you're going before you set out to get there. Take a minute and consider: What's your (or your team's) end goal? Begin with that picture in mind.
- Dave

At first the trail will probably take some getting used to. It's uphill and there are plenty of roots and rocks to trip over. The guide gives us some tips along the way, and we can watch how she's navigating the path. She's traveled it before so she knows what to expect. As we imitate her, we get more comfortable with traveling the path.

Periodically, the guide stops the whole group to let everyone rest. Around a campfire, we drink water, maybe have a light snack, compare notes with the other hikers, and talk about how amazing it will be when we make it to the top. We leave refreshed and ready to continue the journey uphill.

When we finally reach the top of the mountain, everyone celebrates. We admire the view. We reflect on what it took to get here. We enjoy one another's company. Some of us talk about hiking this trail again someday and consider who we might bring along. Who do we know who might really enjoy this? Others consider different paths for future hiking. But most of all at the top of the mountain, we look out over the treetops and enjoy the moment.

The life of a church—a gathering of disciples—is also about getting somewhere. There is a goal, and there are steps we need to take to reach that goal. The Apostle Paul describes the life of faith as a race, and also described how we should run it:

> *Would you ever consider climbing a mountain without a guide? I wouldn't. In fact, I wouldn't know how to begin. A guide is like a coach. He or she asks you the questions to help you discover what you need to know, to make sure you reach the end of your journey.*
>
> *- Dave*

Therefore, since we are surrounded by such a great cloud of witnesses, let us throw off everything that hinders and the sin that so easily entangles. And let us run with perseverance the race marked out for us, fixing our eyes on Jesus, the pioneer and perfecter of faith. For the joy set before him he endured the cross, scorning its shame, and sat down at the right hand of the throne of God. Consider him who endured such opposition from sinners, so that you will not grow weary and lose heart (Heb. 12:1–3).

We are not sitting still. We are going somewhere… together. There are obstacles; there is motivation; there is even an audience. Much perseverance is required. But there is a destination: the throne of God. (Remember Revelation 7? That's where we're going.) Therefore, we need to understand the stages we must go through in order to run this race successfully.

The four stages of the race

Get ready: We prepare for the race. We consider where we're going and whether it's worth the effort. We might need to

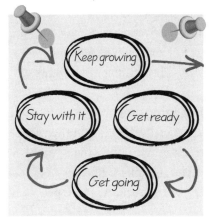

get some new shoes. We might need to get in better condition. We throw off everything that hinders and the sin that entangles.

> Become familiar with the four stages of the race: get ready, get going, stay with it, keep growing. We'll review all four of these repeatedly as we explore the missional journeys ahead.
>
> – Dave

Get going: The shot is fired and we launch off from the starting line with the rest of our teammates. We begin running the race marked out for us, getting a feel for the road. We begin living into our faith more and more, understanding experientially what is required of us. We find our stride.

Stay with it: This is the perseverance part, the part about not growing weary and losing heart. It's a long race. We need encouragement and support—the cheering of the crowd, the sense that others are in this with us. And of course, we need to keep our eyes fixed on Jesus, the author and perfecter of our faith.

Keep growing: There's a good reason we're running this race. Our destination is worth it—the throne of God. But we want to continue returning to take others with us, and help them along this race. Only then will we see people from every nation, tribe, people, and language gathered around the throne with us.

These four stages of the race are what we'll walk through in each of the upcoming chapters. Each chapter outlines a race for us to embark upon and to guide others along:

- Engaging culture
- Forming missional communities
- Developing leadership
- Multiplying movements

Engaging culture means living incarnationally as Jesus did: serving sacrificially, building authentic relationships, and engaging in spiritual transformation. By living in this way, we make disciples of others and become better disciples ourselves. As missional leaders, we can help people learn to engage culture. As more people begin living as Jesus did, we gather together and **begin forming missional communities**. Missional communities—smaller gatherings of disciples—perform all the basic functions of the church, providing support for one another and equipping for ministry. Indeed, from the perspective of many leaders, missional communities are churches. Yet the third and fourth areas remain important, regardless of our philosophy of ministry. **Developing leadership** focuses on sustainable organization and the leadership functions that support the church. And the intentional growth and nurture of these churches are what make up **multiplying movements**.

All four of these together make up the missional journey. The chart below provides a big picture map of the whole journey. This is not a chart you actually fill out, but it shows you the structure of what's unpacked in the rest of the book.

	Engaging Culture	Forming missional communities	Developing leadership	Multiplying movements	
Get ready					
Get going					
Stay with it					
Keep growing					

In the following chapters, we'll take each of these four areas in turn and look at how we, as missional leaders, can best facilitate the missional journey.

In the next chapter we'll dive more deeply into how we can help people engage culture. What do they need to do to get ready to engage culture, to get going doing it, to stay with it, and to keep growing and they and others engage culture?

Journey Guide: Getting there

What's the big picture of a multiplying movement?

Here are some expected core outcomes for each of the four essential journeys:

Engaging culture

- serving the least and the lost
- building redemptive relationships
- praying with and for others
- discerning spiritual openness
- sharing the gospel

Forming communities/churches

- authentic relationships
- sacrificial service
- spiritual transformation
- gathering for worship and prayer
- gift-based ministry
- making more and better disciples

Developing leadership

- mobilizing
- apprenticing (show-how training)
- coaching
- leadership communities
- celebrating successes and learning from experiences
- affirming vision and values
- organizing for further expansion

Multiplying movements

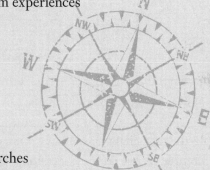

- mobilizing apostolic leaders
- sending ministry teams
- crossing cultural barriers
- multiplying disciples, groups, and churches
- new movements starting new movements

Discussion questions: for you and your team

1. How do you understand the metaphor of the journey? What implications does it have for us?
2. Using a whiteboard, ask your team for ideas. What might work well at the...
   - "get ready" stage?
   - "get going" stage?
   - "stay with it" stage?
   - "keep growing" stage?

Guided prayer: for you and your team

Ask God for:

- A listening heart
- Discernment
- A humble spirit
- The will to be obedient
- Continued renewal of the vision

Planning questions: for you and your coach

1. What important lessons have you learned so far?
2. What opportunities like ahead for you?
3. What are your next steps forward?

To do list: action points to implement

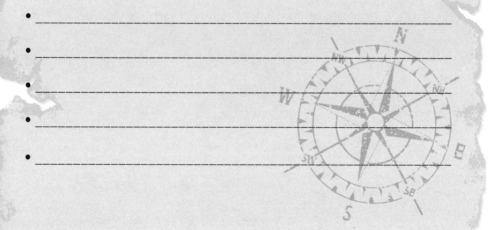

- _____

- _____

- _____

- _____

- _____

Chapter 5

Engaging culture

In an era when Christian spirituality is often defined by avoiding the temptations of worldliness, what does it mean to engage with the world? Shouldn't we be concerned about "becoming polluted by the world" and "avoiding even the appearance of evil"?

Generally speaking, when Christians today strive to "avoid even the appearance of evil," we avoid making any appearance at all. We then lose any chance to share the good news of the gospel in any way people can understand. Instead of the city on a hill giving light to all around us, we hide our light.

In an attempt to correct this problem, then, some of us have swung the pendulum to the other end, advocating hanging out in bars in order to demonstrate our relevance. In some cases this means we become absorbed completely into the world, becoming indistinguishable from it, and therefore equally unable to give light to those around us.

The apostle Paul addressed this issue of who to associate with. He wasn't saying not to associate with immoral unbelievers, but immoral believers.

I wrote to you in my letter not to associate with sexually immoral people—not at all meaning the people of this world who are immoral, or the greedy and swindlers, or idolaters. In that case you would have to leave this world. But now I am writing to you that you must not associate with anyone who claims to be a brother or sister but is sexually immoral or greedy, an idolater or slanderer, a drunkard or swindler. Do not even eat with such people. What business is it of mine to judge those outside the church? (1 Cor. 5:9–12).

With unbelievers, we are to be agents of transformation—salt and light and good news in the world. Just like Jesus was. In the gospels, we see him interacting with tax collectors, women, and prostitutes. We see him being called a drunkard. We see him attending weddings and parties and having dinner in people's homes.

We also see Jesus saying difficult things that people did not want to hear, turning people's worldviews upside down, giving both grace and challenge according to what the situation warranted. We see him standing out and being different, but in a good way.

One of the obstacles to engaging the culture is "extractionalism." Extractionalism is moving new Christians out of relationship with nonbelievers in the culture, in order to foster new relationships almost exclusively within the church. As Tom Clegg notes, "If you don't have friends outside the church, there's something wrong with you—and your version of Christianity." This chapter will show you how to engage the culture!
*   - Dave*

Engaging culture is about more than just going to bars. It means being where the people are, living among them, getting to know them, letting them get to know us. It also means shining the light of Jesus into dark places bringing hope and transformation. When we meet people on their turf, allowing them to really know us—including our spirituality—that's when we find people who are curious about God and open to him. That's when people choose to follow Jesus, and begin following him out of their own culture, not ours. Simple incarnational living means bringing Jesus *into* the culture.

One follower of Jesus rides his Harley with an outlaw motorcycle club. He's not an official patch member but has earned the right to participate and be heard in a fairly exclusive community.

What does it mean to engage culture?

Engaging culture simply means living incarnationally among the people with whom God has placed us. We are to live in such a way that shows Jesus to them. Just as Jesus said, "My Father is always at his work to this very day, and I too am working" (John 5:17), our works are to line up with and illuminate what God is already doing. God is always at work—even if we see just a spark—and we are to do what we see him doing. We bring hope and transformation by joining him in his work.

As Brandon Hatmaker puts it in his book *Barefoot Church*, "You can't engage culture without engaging the needs of culture." Who are the people God has placed us among? What are their needs? How can we know them? How can we help them? How can we be Jesus to them? What are we hearing from God? What actions can we take?

When we live with these kinds of questions in mind, we are living incarnationally as Jesus did, engaging with the culture around us in meaningful ways. Anyone who starts by engaging a need is engaging culture well.

We engage culture through the three core elements of the missional journey: sacrificial service, authentic relationships, and spiritual transformation. The result is changed lives, changed communities, and changed neighborhoods.

All believers, regardless of giftedness or abilities, are called to engage culture. This journey is for everyone. It's the essential DNA of all the rest of the journeys. Even high-level leaders focusing on developing leaders or multiplying movements can never leave this first journey behind. All missional ministry—however large in scale—starts with individuals deciding

These are some great questions to discuss with your team. Grab a large piece of poster paper and trace a body on it. Then begin writing answers to these questions on the poster. Begin developing a visual image of the people God is bringing into your life and how you can be Jesus to them.

- Dave

> Christians have been transformed to have a transforming influence in the world. God has designed the church for this purpose. Charles Van Engen notes that "the collection of transformed individuals creates a transformed culture."
>
> – Dave

to live incarnationally within the culture around them. No one is exempt and no one can lead where they haven't been. Engaging the culture is foundational to the rest of the missional journey. When we lose touch with the culture, we lose the right to speak into it.

How can we help people engage culture?

In this chapter, we'll outline the journey of how we can help people engage culture. What are the starting points? The milestones? How can we help people stay on track? What kind of results can we expect to see? By walking through the stages of the race below, we can guide people along the journey toward engaging culture.

Get ready

Like any exercise—or in this case, "race-training"—program, the hardest part is getting started. Here are a few tips for getting ready:

Recognize that not everyone wants to run this race. Not everyone who calls themselves Christian wants to live incarnationally. Some who claim to follow Jesus in fact care very little about the things that Jesus cares about. As a missional church planter, you'll need to recognize that not everybody is going to come along with you—because not everybody wants to.

Start with those who are receptive. You don't need everyone, and you don't even need very many people—just a handful who are receptive and willing to go on the adventure. As you begin exploring the possibilities, you'll find that there are plenty of people who are willing to talk about serving, but significantly fewer who are willing to do it. You'll also likely find that new followers of Jesus are the most receptive. Ask God about who could join you in this missional journey. Look for people in whom God is already working. Don't focus on those who aren't willing to engage, even if they seem especially gifted. Focus on those who are willing, and watch how God equips them for the adventure

Expect an uphill climb. Particularly if you're starting with an existing group of Christians, it's difficult to nudge them out of the Christian subculture. Many long-time believers are most comfortable around other Christians. However, hanging out only with other Christians removes them from their natural spheres of influence. Know that you may encounter some steep resistance—even among those who eventually decide to join.

Orient people. Those who are interested in engaging culture need some idea of what to expect. What will this journey be like? What will be required of them? Tell them. But you'll also need to show them. Hearing about something and seeing it are two different things. Do both. Consider the people you're working with. Who needs to get oriented? Who needs to get exposed? How can we most effectively do that? A good orientation process should provide people with a clear understanding of what it means to engage culture, an intentional process of some kind to commit to, and a supportive community to walk alongside them on this journey.

> As part of your orientation, take a missional tour of your community with your team. Go for a walk or take a drive, with the intention of seeing your community from a different perspective. Spend the entire day observing, learning, and seeing what God sees when he looks at your city.
> - What breaks God's heart?
> - What gives God joy?
> - What could God use here?
> - What would God like to clean up?
> - What is God saying to us?
> Spend some time afterward debriefing your "walk/drive-through," praying over the things God's revealed and how he might want you to respond to those things.
> - Dave

Set an example. If you won't do it, they won't do it. If you're in positions of leadership, people will look to you to see what you value. Expect people to pay much more attention to your actions than to your words. The beginning of helping others engage culture is us engaging culture. Without that foundational piece in place, any broader impact won't take hold. So consider: What are you doing personally? You don't have to be great at it—you just have to be living it and modeling it. A few years back I was in a mountain biking group with people who weren't followers of Jesus. Mountain biking is something I do anyway, but I chose to do it intentionally alongside people who weren't believers.

Invite people to join you. As you begin to engage culture, find ways to do it alongside others. We don't have to bring everyone along, but if we look around there's almost certainly someone who'd like to serve and engage alongside us. Once someone is with us, it's a whole lot easier to live this way, and to more easily identify additional opportunities to serve alongside others.

Help people to be friends to others. Spiritual transformation means: Who we are, and how God is changing our lives, makes us salt and light to other people. But it also implies that we have authentic relationships in the first place. Many Christians need to first learn how to be a good friend and how to be a good neighbor. There's no artificial "us vs. them." Help people learn how to be friends to others. Then, while God is changing their lives, people they're in relationship with will notice how they live. Think about the coffee shop where you go every morning. You're a regular; people know you. Because of this, you have the opportunity to develop authentic relationships there—with baristas, with other regulars—and begin to be salt and light to them.

Encourage people to serve. There are a million and one different ways to serve. One man started walking around his relatively affluent neighborhood once a week, collecting canned food donations from his neighbors. They were glad for the opportunity to give and he made it easy for them. In this way, he was also able to build relationships with many of his neighbors.

Identify people to invest in. Among those people who indicate receptivity to missional living, some will be willing to go the extra mile in living it out. Look for those who "get" missional living, and who are willing to take risks. These are the people you need to invest in through coaching, discipling, or mentoring. It's through them that you'll see missional transformation taking root.

The biggest issue at this stage of the race is just getting started…. even if everyone's not on board. Even if not everything works. Even if you're starting small. You just need to start somewhere. Engage your culture as best you can, become part of it, establish relationships, and serve those you encounter. From there, invite others to serve alongside you and see what God does.

Where do you start? One place you can start is with listening prayer, walking around your neighborhood. Make a list of the places you already go and the things you already do. Then, ask God to show you what's on his heart. Ask yourself:

- What do you like to do?
- How can you do that with others who don't already follow Jesus?
- What needs do you see?
- How can you serve?

When my coach was helping me figure out how I could live more missionally, he asked, "How can you free up one hour a week?" Then he asked, "How can you use that one hour?" Even if it's simply an hour spent in prayer, it matters. After a while, we moved up to three hours. "How can you free up three hours?"

> A simple question to ask of your team is: Who do we know that has a need? Then together meet that need. Imagine what would happen if every small group you started took time to ask this question every time they met
> – Dave

"How can you use those three hours?" God can do a lot with whatever amount of time you give him. So give him that time, and get ready to do what he wants to do with it.

Get going

This stage is exactly what it sounds like: moving past the starting line. We've prepared, we have people who've joined us, and we're out on the track. Now we learn how to navigate along the track.

The main challenge of this stage is the whole "making mistakes" thing. What if we throw a party and it doesn't go well? What if we serve a meal to the homeless and don't know what to say? What if we volunteer in a recovery home and we can't figure out how to connect with the people? We instinctively recognize that if we try something new—especially something that's not on our own turf—we may not look so good. And that feels awkward, particularly for people in positions of leadership. It's one thing to look good while preaching. It's another to have a real conversation with someone who thinks very differently than you do. Don't allow your fear of failure to block your progress. Give yourselves— and others—the freedom to make mistakes. It's the only way to learn.

The good news is this: We don't have to be good at incarnational living and engaging culture. We just have to dive in and start doing it. Our skills will increase as we get more practice, but that's not the point. The point is to believe in something enough to do it— even at the risk of looking bad, making a fool of yourself, or trying something new that may or may not work. Here are a few ideas to get you going:

- Get to know some people who aren't already followers of Jesus. How might you meet those people in a natural way? Join a book club, a PTA, a volleyball team… something that you enjoy that provides natural relational connections.

- Volunteer somewhere. If you're on staff at church, that doesn't mean you can't volunteer somewhere else: a school, a treatment center, a battered women's shelter, a food pantry.

- Tell personal stories about what you're involved in. That will help cast vision for missional living, and when people hear what you're doing, it will encourage them to get involved, too.

What are some concrete ways we can support others who are in the "get going" stage of engaging culture?

Show people how. We'll need to model what engaging culture looks like for people. Give them opportunities to watch you engaging culture. Be present when they are engaging culture. Use the show-how training model that Jesus used with his disciples:

- I do, you watch
- I do, you help
- You do, I help
- You do, I watch
- You do, someone else watches

Keep in mind that as we're interacting with people, we'll need to dialogue with them at each stage, to help them reflect on what they're learning.

> *Many churches will end up consuming all the volunteer time their members have available to focus on internal ministry. This leaves little or no time to serve outside the church. Value volunteers wherever they serve. Start training people to serve outside the church. Commission and send people to volunteer with other organizations.*
>
> *- Dave*

Ask questions. Taking a coaching posture can be incredibly helpful, even if you're not a formally trained coach. Coaching is just coming alongside people, listening, and asking them where God wants them to go next. Simple coaching questions include:

- Who are you reaching?
- What do they need?
- Where do you sense God tugging on your heart lately?
- What actions might God be leading you toward?

Help them reflect and listen to the Spirit. It's amazing what can happen if we just take the time to slow down and reflect with people—to think about what God is up to—then take one further step that makes it just a little more intentional. There's so much joy when we come alongside others to help them process those ah-ha moments of realization, and then help them follow through on what God's revealing to them.

Show grace. Keep supporting, keep praying, and allow room for growth. *"Your love has given me great joy and encouragement, because you, brother, have refreshed the hearts of the Lord's people"* (Philem. 1:7).

Stay with it

As we and those we are leading learn to increasingly engage culture, we'll be in for an adventurous ride. We'll run across unexpected opportunities, sudden roadblocks, and puzzling quandaries. This is the season of both challenging and supporting people along their missional journey.

I use the examples of rubber bands and shoelaces. With rubber bands, no stretch equals no growth—but if we stretch people too far, they break. Shoelaces, on the other hand, need to be tied together to function—just as people need to be tied together in relational networks in order to function well. The question for us as leaders is how we can give people the appropriate amount of stretch, and at the same time tie them together for support.

Here are some ideas for stretching and supporting your people:

Provide ongoing coaching. Every person is different. There's no way each person will need the same amount of stretch at the same time. To know who needs what, we need to stay in relationship with them. We can't personally be in relationship with everyone at the same time, but we can provide ongoing coaching for people involved in our ministry. Together with their coach, each person can create an individualized plan of stretch and support, depending on how they're serving and what's going on in their lives at the time.

Provide connections with peers. Many of us are tempted to skip leader gatherings. They can sound unnecessary, like an optional social gathering. But we need these gatherings. They're relational, but they're also intentional. They provide space for sharing how we're doing with incarnational living—room to share the struggles and the joys, and the opportunity to hear the stories of others. We need peer gatherings more than we think we do. They provide support, fresh energy, new ideas, and renewed vision—that sense of being part of something bigger.

Help them become students of the culture. Just as someone who plans to move overseas engages in research about the culture, we also must become students of the culture around us. It may be the culture we grew up within or it may just be where we find ourselves right now. Either way, we need to become intentional students. Where do people live, work, and hang out? What do they value? How do they organize themselves socially? What are their needs? How could they be served sacrificially? Answering questions like these can't be done in a library. We have to get to know people, observe them, ask questions, and become part of the fabric of the culture.

> In the Old Testament, the men of Issachar "understood the times and knew what Israel should do." Apparently, they had an awareness of what was going on around them. But not only did they understand the times, they also knew what should be done. Become a student of your community. Understand the times. Know what the church should do.
> - Dave

Help them look for responsiveness. Within every group, some people will be more spiritually responsive than others. Every group will also have some individuals who serve as "persons of peace." These are influential people who are known in their community. They could be anyone from the town philanthropist to the gang leader to the stay-at-home mom who knows everyone. They are connected, and some are spiritually responsive. Authentic relationships with these people can be the key to starting whole new missional communities through their preexisting social structures. They are the seedbeds of spiritual transformation. As we lead people who are already engaging culture, we'll need to help them become aware of the people of peace who cross their paths.

> A church in Indianapolis planted a new church in an apartment complex across the street from their church building because God brought them to a person of peace. Rather than trying to pull people out of their social structure to "come to church," they decided to bring the church to the apartment complex.
> - Dave

Remember the "authentic" in authentic relationships. People are never a means to an end. We don't live incarnationally so that we can make disciples. We live incarnationally simply because Jesus told us to serve. Of those we serve, some will be spiritually receptive and want to know more. From those people, we make disciples.

Identify the skills people need. Only after people begin engaging culture will they become aware of the skills they need to develop. Some skills may be more traditional, such as small-group facilitation skills. Other skills may involve specific types of service needed to provide for the community. Others may need to work on conflict-resolution skills or basic social skills. We never know what we need until we get started. Once you've identified the necessary skills, find ways to help people develop them.

Help one another become disciples. As you live incarnationally and missionally, engaging the culture around you, you'll need to be intentional about discipleship. You'll need to think through what a disciple is, and what he or she looks like in your particular missional context. As you develop disciples, what outcomes or behaviors are you looking for? True discipleship is holistic, reaching the heart, the hands, and the head. A disciple:

- Loves God
- Love and serves others
- Makes other disciples

After you've thought through the specific behaviors of a disciple, think through how to be intentional about developing those behaviors. There are many different approaches and strategies for cultivating discipleship in others. Consider what kinds of processes and tools may work best in your particular context and adapt accordingly. Making disciples is not an individualistic activity—just as incarnational living is not an individualistic activity—but is done in the context of missional community.

Here's a simple activity that will focus your disciple-making efforts. With your team, consider what a follower of Jesus needs to know, be, and do. Make a list or chart. Then work together to help develop these areas, in your own lives and in the lives of those you're discipling.
- Dave

The key to the stretching and supporting is consistency: just stay with it. Keep on engaging culture; keep on praying for one another; keep on asking one another questions to help each other stay on track. As we journey together, we'll need to continue listening to the Holy Spirit and changing course when necessary. Support one another in prayer, encourage one another, and hold one another accountable: *"And let us consider how we may spur one another on toward love and good deeds, not giving up meeting together, as some are in the habit of doing, but encouraging one another—and all the more as you see the Day approaching"* (Heb. 10:24–25).

Keep growing

As we and those we lead increasingly engage culture and grow in discipleship, we'll begin to see God working. Every context is different; some places see slower growth than others, but God is always present and working in some way. Jesus explained the parable of the sower along these lines:

> *"Listen then to what the parable of the sower means: When anyone hears the message about the kingdom and does not understand it, the evil one comes and snatches away what was sown in their heart. This is the seed sown along the path. The seed falling on rocky ground refers to someone who hears the word and at once receives it with joy. But since they have no root, they last only a short time. When trouble or persecution comes because of the word, they quickly fall away. The seed falling among the thorns refers to someone who hears the word, but the worries of this life and the deceitfulness of wealth choke the word, making it unfruitful. But the seed falling on good soil refers to someone who hears the word and understands it. This is the one who produces a crop, yielding a hundred, sixty or thirty times what was sown"* (Matt. 13:18–23).

Our task, then, is to look for the good soil. Where is the transforming message of the gospel taking root and growing? Where do we most see the movement of the Holy Spirit? From that point, how can we focus our efforts to expand upon what God is blessing?

Remind yourself and your people regularly that new followers of Jesus are the seeds of new missional communities. This is how we bridge from engaging culture to forming missional communities (the subject of the next chapter). Gratitude leads to a desire to share. When we have so much, how can we help spread some of those spiritual riches to others? Grace multiplies.

> *Therefore, as God's chosen people, holy and dearly loved, clothe yourselves with compassion, kindness, humility, gentleness and patience. Bear with each other and forgive one another if any of you has a grievance against someone. Forgive as the Lord forgave you. And over all these virtues put on love, which binds them all together in perfect unity.*

> *Let the peace of Christ rule in your hearts, since as members of one body you were called to peace. And be thankful. Let the message of Christ dwell among you richly as you teach and admonish one another with all wisdom through psalms, hymns, and songs from the Spirit, singing to God with gratitude in your hearts. And whatever you do, whether in word or deed, do it all in the name of the Lord Jesus, giving thanks to God the Father through him (Col. 3:12–17).*

When we consider metaphors such as a journey or a race in light of light of engaging culture, the destination portion is in some ways a misnomer. When it comes to living as Jesus lived, we never really arrive and we never really cross the finish line here on earth. But there is a point when we feel established on the journey. A sense of peace comes when we feel deep down that we're doing what we were meant to be doing and living according to the way we were designed. That's a time for celebration—a celebration of gratitude to God for setting us on this path that we'd never have been able to travel without the help of his Spirit all along the way.

It's also a time for considering who else might want to join us on this journey of engaging culture, living incarnationally, and becoming disciples. Who might want to run alongside us? Now that we are familiar with the route and some of its twists and turns, we can serve as a guide for others. Their experience of it will differ from our own, but we can still keep pace alongside them and help them discover what God has for them.

Finally, the destination is a place for reflection. What are you hearing from God? What are you sensing he has for you next? Sometimes there's another race to be run in addition to engaging culture. We'll look at some of those journeys in subsequent chapters.

Engaging culture means meeting people where they're at and engaging with the realities of the needs that are out there. Communidad Mosaico in Mexico City is one organization that excels in engaging culture. They have a vision for transformation among the urban poor. Their list of strategic interventions reflects the breadth and range of their holistic ministry:

- Comunidades de Shalom—Planting Holistic Churches
- Nehemiah Challenge—Discipling Our Cities
- Centro Renovar—Spiritual, Emotional and Physical Renewal for Leaders
- Project Fortaleza—Strengthening Civil Society
- Project ProSalud—Building Healthy Communities
- Project ACJU—Youth as Agents of Change
- Project ProNiñez—Holistic Development for Children
- GruposVida—Emotional Recovery for Hurting People
- InKrea—Business & Economic Development

These various facets of Communidad Mosaico have resulted in community health initiatives, kids' nutrition programs, youth life skills and leadership development training, Bible studies, homework clubs, house churches, and women's emotional recovery groups. They are meeting the culture where it's at, addressing both physical and spiritual needs in the community.

Engaging culture in the ways Jesus engaged culture is the first and most foundational journey; it's connected to all the rest.

As for everyone who comes to me and hears my words and puts them into practice, I will show you what they are like. They are like a man building a house, who dug down deep and laid the foundation on rock. When a flood came, the torrent struck that house but could not shake it, because it was well built. But the one who hears my words and does not put them into practice is like a man who built a house on the ground without a foundation. The moment the torrent struck that house, it collapsed and its destruction was complete" (Luke 6:47–49).

If you're a missional leader or planter, this passage is particularly important for you. Your life in Christ, and your obedience to him, is the rock. All the rest of what you do will be built on that foundation. And if the rock is really sand, the whole ministry will crumble.

As we live incarnationally as Jesus did, we'll begin seeing the fruit: authentic relationships, redemptive acts, sacrificial service, and transformation—not only personal transformation, but also transformation in the communities around us. Together, all of this will lead to the formation of more missional communities.

The man who built on the rock and the man who built on the sand both heard Jesus' words. The difference was putting what Jesus said into practice. It's easy to know what Jesus says to do. It's a totally different thing to actually obey it. Jesus says that making disciples isn't just teaching what he commanded. Making disciples requires teaching to obey. If you aren't obeying Jesus yourself, you'll have a difficult time teaching others to obey. As you reflect on this chapter - what does obeying Jesus look like for you?

- Dave

Journey Guide: Engaging culture

Checklist: You are here

engaging culture
- serving the least and the lost
- building redemptive relationships
- praying with and for others
- discerning spiritual openness
- sharing the gospel

forming communities/churches

developing leadership

multiplying movements

Discussion questions: for you and your team

- What are you already doing?
- What's going well?
- What do you hear God saying to you?
- What reflections do you have about this chapter?

Guided prayer: for you and your team

Spend time as a team in prayer. Ask God the following questions, allowing time for people to respond aloud in prayer:

- How can we engage the culture around us?
- Who would you have us reach?
- How can we serve as Jesus served?
- What needs to change in us?

Action planning guide

"Engaging culture" coaching questions:

- How are you serving the least and the lost?
- How are you building redemptive relationships?
- How are you praying with and for others?
- How are you discerning spiritual openness?
- How are you sharing the gospel?

Based on where you currently are in engaging your culture, work through the following questions and action steps together with your team:

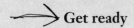 **Get ready**

Action points:

- Orient your people to what engaging culture looks like
- Study your community/neighborhood
- Listen and ask questions
- Pray together
- Set an example of being a good friend and neighbor

Questions to discuss with your team:

- Who are the lost here?
- What is the good news to them?

⟶ **Get going**

Action points:

- Plan a get-together
- Start conversations
- Volunteer somewhere
- Tell stories

Questions to discuss with your team:

- How can we serve those around us?
- What's one small thing you can do this week?

⟶ **Stay with it**

Action points:

- Create an environment for regular reflective conversation
- Continue to learn the culture
- Look for persons of peace
- Keep being authentic
- Make disciples

Questions to discuss with your team:

- Where are you sensing spiritual openness?
- What new skills might you need to develop?

⟶ **Keep growing**

Action points:

- Express gratitude
- Remember that new followers of Jesus are the seeds of new missional communities
- Help others develop authentic relationships
- Guide others toward engaging culture

Questions to discuss with your team:

- What can we celebrate?
- What are you sensing God has for us next?

Chapter 6

Forming missional communities

In our last chapter we talked about engaging culture—building relationships, discovering the needs of people, and serving sacrificially. This chapter assumes we've put some of the things we've learned into practice. We know our neighbors. We begin to know the friends of our neighbors. We may be volunteering at nonprofit organizations, alongside people who aren't followers of Jesus, and have built relationships with them as well. In short, we've become part of the fabric of the community around us.

As we begin living in this way—incarnationally, as Jesus himself was incarnational—we will begin to notice people around us who are spiritually responsive, and we can start engaging them in the conversation of how to follow Jesus. As we engage in those spiritual conversations, we also begin keeping our eyes open for that "person of peace"—someone of influence who, if he or she decides to follow Jesus, will impact his or her whole network. The person of peace opens up the doors to others.

> You may wonder if a missional community is just another way to refer to a small group or Bible study. It's really not. A missional community is group of people following Jesus together with a commitment to sacrificial service, authentic relationships, and spiritual transformation.
>
> - Dave

As people come to Jesus we form communities of Jesus-followers—called churches in the New Testament. These are disciple-making communities where people engage all the functions of the church:

worshipping, edifying one another, serving together, using spiritual gifts, and experiencing transformation. As more people come to faith, new opportunities arise for forming new communities.

That's the story of this chapter: forming missional communities. And that story starts with faith conversations, helping people along the journey of faith, and looking for people of peace.

Faith conversations

There are a lot of very kind people out there who are networked into the community. Sometimes the Mormon guy or the Buddhist guy is the nicest person on the street, shoveling everyone's walks when it snows. Living incarnationally and missionally as followers of Jesus brings something different to the equation: the power of spiritual transformation. We understand what it is like to have the Spirit of God transforming our lives, and we have the ability to share that good news with others.

So how do we do that? We listen. We ask questions. Then we figure out how to best come alongside others on their spiritual journey. A two-way flow of communication will help us better understand what people's needs are. We can provide prayer, support, resources, connections to other people, or a listening ear as we respond to what God is doing. We can share our own stories about Jesus and how he has changed us.

Many of us are good at responding to physical or practical needs, but not so good at responding to spiritual needs. Others of us are just the opposite. The truth is, it takes both. Words without actions are dead. And the good news unshared isn't good news. What spiritual needs are we aware of in those around us? As we invest honestly and authentically in relationships with people who don't know Jesus, at some point spiritual needs will arise.

Hugh Halter, a friend of mine and a missional church leader, built a friendship with his yoga instructor. When his instructor heard that Hugh had a book coming out, she wanted to borrow a copy. After she read it, she told him, "I grew up Catholic and Baptist, but I've never heard anyone talk about Jesus like that. Could we get together for coffee sometime so I could hear more about this?"

Sometimes people just enter into a season of wondering about spiritual things. Other times, they become aware of spiritual needs during a time of life crisis. An elderly woman and her family were evacuated from East Houston during a hurricane. The family who hosted them was part of a missional church and shared the gospel message. This woman came to faith at 85 years old.

In the context of dialoguing with people, we'll understand more about what their life situations are—and what their spiritual needs are. We'll hear their questions and see where people need to understand more about Jesus. Sharing the story of Jesus goes far beyond handing out a tract. It's a potentially complex story that needs to be clarified so people can understand it. Don't be worried too much about people understanding all the nuances of the gospel message at once; for all of us, our understanding of Jesus continues to grow throughout our lifetimes. But we do need to figure out a way that shows Jesus to people who aren't quite sure what to make of him. We can simply tell the story of Jesus in our own words, and usually that will also include sharing about some of our own experience with God, as we dialogue.

Helping people along the journey of faith

What if someone says yes, they want to follow Jesus? What then? It's easy to get buried in "shoulds": church attendance, making amends, learning how to do devotions. But especially at first, much of that misses the central point of spiritual transformation: forgiveness and relationship. It's a celebration! Like the father seeing his prodigal son approach from a long way off, God is rejoicing. How people start off in their life of faith has a big impact down the road, so be sure to focus on

Whether you've been following Jesus for a long time or just getting started, you have some favorite stories about Jesus. Which stories impact you the most? Which stories draw you toward him? Write out a list of your favorite stories. Read them again and practice telling them in your own words. Then choose one to share with someone this week.

- Dave

what's truly important. There'll be time for all the rest later.

What do people need to just get started in their new relationship with God? Just the basics. Whatever we do, if we want to make holistic disciples we'll want to include authentic relationships, sacrificial service, and spiritual transformation. Other issues to consider at the very beginning include prayer, baptism, helping people share their faith, and connecting them to the larger body of Christ. They don't need connection to the whole body at once—in some cases that will serve to cut them off from their own natural community. A good starting point is a relationship with just a few individuals who are further along the journey of faith.

One new believer confessed to his community group that he was curious about scripture and had purchased *The Bible for Dummies*—desiring to be discipled in more depth but without being pulled out of his current context and relationships. Some of the men from his community group decided to help by forming an online daily Bible study group that journaled via email. A year later, this man writes with insight and spiritual depth, and yet has maintained a seamless primary connection with his original relational community.

> A key to orienting new disciples is found in Jesus' words to his disciples in Matthew 28. He instructed his disciples to teach "to obey everything I have commanded." Believe it or not, Christians aren't good at this. We teach to know—but not necessarily to obey. As you work with new followers of Jesus, teach them to do what Jesus says.
> - Dave

What help can we provide as others begin to follow Jesus? We may want to connect people to a Life Transformation Group (LTG). This is a group of two to four people who gather together regularly to read scripture, pray, and help each other grow. The appendix of this book contains a basic format for how LTGs work, and can be downloaded for free at *www.loganleadership.com.*

We'll also want to provide some type of orientation to the journey of faith for those who are new to it. As we start new believers off on the journey of faith, we'll need to think through what we mean when we say disciple. Who is a disciple? What does he or she do? What behaviors will we see from disciples? Whatever resources we use as we help new believers become established in their faith will need to reflect our beliefs about becoming disciples. Several of these resources—including the *Journey Together Now Guides*—can be found at ***www.loganleadership.com***.

Looking for the person of peace

As new believers come into the faith, we'll want to look particularly for people of peace. The Apostle Paul and his team ran across numerous people of peace. One of them, Lydia, is described in Acts 16:

> On the Sabbath we went outside the city gate to the river, where we expected to find a place of prayer. We sat down and began to speak to the women who had gathered there. One of those listening was a woman from the city of Thyatira named Lydia, a dealer in purple cloth. She was a worshiper of God. The Lord opened her heart to respond to Paul's message. When she and the members of her household were baptized, she invited us to her home. "If you consider me a believer in the Lord," she said, "come and stay at my house." And she persuaded us (Acts 16:13–15).

These are people who, upon coming to faith, open up whole new networks to the gospel of Jesus. Contemporary examples include a police officer who became a believer and brought most of his coworkers to faith, a woman who was well connected in her neighborhood, and a music school student who was well respected by his peers. Some new believers have the influence to reach their entire network with the gospel message. When they get excited about something, they bring all of their friends along.

One pastor in Australia was working with a surfing community, and trying to figure out how to build a deeper connection into this particular subculture. His coach asked him to try to identify the person of peace. The pastor was able to identify that person immediately. It was someone he'd been thinking of trying to draw into his church. The coach suggested that the pastor might disciple this man personally, while allowing him to maintain his primary relational connection with the others in the surfing community. The pastor did that—and one year later, that person of peace had led dozens of those other surfers to faith in Jesus; they even

The temptation for a missional leader is to start a missional community with a group of Christians that he or she already has relationship with. Don't do this. Start your missional community with non-Christians or new Christians. Train the Christians you know to start their own missional communities. Then provide the support they need through coaching, in order to multiply missional communities all over the place.

— Dave

had formed their own missional community.

Persons of peace are important because they represent the bridge between engaging culture and forming missional communities. They are the bedrock upon which new missional communities are formed.

Every believer is part of the body of Christ. Whenever someone comes to faith, ask the question, "Where is the rest of the body?" Each new believer represents the seeds of a new missional community. Assume that every new follower of Jesus might be the beginning of a new faith community. As new believers come to faith, we face the question of whether to fold them into our community or help them start their own. Let the default choice be to start a new one whenever possible. Help new believers reach their oikos (which literally means "household," but often extends to one's circle of relationship), and find the person of peace who can form a new community around them.

People of peace are where we see the breakthroughs. They form new communities of disciples who live life together as the people of God. They build authentic relationships both inside and outside the community of faith, serve sacrificially, and see powerful transformation take place in people's lives.

Now we have a picture in our minds of how these communities are formed. Now what? If we want to start a missional community, what do we actually do? How can we help a community of people live out—on a day-to-day, week-to-week basis—the spiritual realities of the Kingdom of God?

How do we...
>   ... live life together?
>   ... help each other become more like Jesus?
>   ... worship?
>   ... release people into their spiritual gifts?
>   ... organize for effective action?
>   ... help others become disciples?

Below, we'll provide the basics of what's needed to facilitate a missional community, or to walk alongside others as they do so.

So what do we do? What are these missional communities supposed to look like?

There are so many ways to gather as a missional community, but here are the basic components: sacrificial serving, authentic relationship, and spiritual transformation. Yes, the same three elements that make up the discipleship process make up a missional community. Make sure all three are included in your gathering times. For most groups it feels most familiar to focus on just one or two of these areas, but remember—it's not a missional community unless it's hitting all of these areas.

You may be wondering what to do when you meet as a missional community. How do you keep from becoming just a small group or Bible study? That's a great question! Read on... and start using some of these ideas in your gatherings.

- Dave

Here are some ideas for each element to get you started, but feel free to get creative:

Sacrificial serving

You're not just a social gathering; you're on a mission. Remind people of that every time you gather. Spend time talking about sacrificial serving when you gather as a missional community. Ask:
- What needs do you or others have?
- How can we meet those needs?

Then plan together how you, as a missional community, will take action that week. Encourage one another in the use of spiritual gifts. Do you know the two best ways to discover spiritual gifts? One is to get the perspective of others who know you well. The other is to try different types of service and see how God seems to be working through you.

Authentic relationship

If you've been in many small groups, you've probably discovered that community for the sake of community doesn't hold up well over time. For community to be authentic, it needs to be about something beyond itself. Remind yourselves of this during your sharing time. In addition to questions like, "How are you doing? How was your week?" try going a little deeper. Ask:

- How did you experience God this week?
- What opportunities did you have to be the hands and feet of Jesus?

Another way to incorporate serving into your missional community is to adopt a school or a specific project in your neighborhood. As you gather, take time to pray and plan. A regular time to serve a specific group each month will not only keep you outwardly focused; it will also become an important part of your discipleship process. It's also a great way to include others who haven't yet committed to following Jesus.

- Dave

Sharing experiences, successes, failures—and everything in between—will exponentially increase the level of authenticity in your missional community.

As a leader, your transparency and openness will help the entire missional community experience a greater sense of transparency. Don't act like you've got it all together—you don't. Share and support one another. And, pray for one another.

- Dave

Pray for one another, and make sure that prayer goes beyond physical problems and needs. Pray for emotional healing, engagement in service, the finding of calling, and forgiveness. Allow your prayers to get real, and to go beyond the surface of life.

Spiritual transformation

There are lots of ways to focus on spiritual transformation. Certainly, reading scripture together and seeking to understand how to apply it to your lives is a great place to start. Try letting different people facilitate the discussion each week. Here are some helpful questions to get conversation started:

- What did you like about what we just read?
- What didn't you like?
- Was there anything you didn't understand?
- What did you learn about God?

When it comes to scripture study, one thing to remember is Jesus' instruction of teaching others to obey. It's not about content or knowledge, but about how you apply it. Share with each other what happened when you obeyed Jesus this past week, and how you intend to obey Jesus this week. Consider asking each other:

Try forming personal applications that begin with the words, "I will." This simple phrasing isn't just semantics. It will increase each person's intentionality to do something that week.
- Dave

- How did you apply what you learned last week? What happened?
- How will you apply what you learned this week?

These questions go beyond Bible study and beyond cognitive understanding—they're about doing something in obedience to Jesus.

If you want a real missional community, one that doesn't fall back into the familiar rut of "just a Bible study" or "just a small group,"

To prioritize all three of these components (sacrificial service, authentic relationships, spiritual transformation) give equal time for each. That time may be inside or outside of regular group meetings, but aim for making it roughly equal over the course of any given month. That creates a rhythm of life.
- Dave

you will have to make time for all three areas into your gatherings. If it doesn't have sacrificial service, it's not a missional community. If it skips over authentic relationships or spiritual transformation, it's not a missional community either. Living this way together means we share all facets of what it means to be church.

Get ready

As in any portion of the missional journey, knowing what to expect at the outset is essential. If a leader is expecting a nice group of people to come together, fellowship with one another, then go home, a missional community is probably not what he or she wants to lead. The expectations and the reality will be too far apart. However, if the leader wants to lead a group of people journeying together with one another toward ongoing spiritual transformation, that's a missional community.

So for those considering forming missional communities: What do they need to do to prepare? What do they need to know in advance?

Every missional community will be a little bit different, but here are some topics that should be addressed at the front end of the journey. Work through these with potential missional community leaders, so they know what to expect. But remember: You don't have to cover these all exhaustively right now. These issues can be dealt with in more depth later on an as-needed basis.

If potential leaders think through these types of issues and questions beforehand, they'll have a clearer idea of where they're going, and of what they want their missional community to be and do. The establishment of coaching relationships, as well as peer groups for missional community leaders, is also best done at this early point in the process. People seeking to form and lead missional communities will need the support of both coaches and peers.

Issue	Key Question
The definition of a missional community	What are we?
The functions and outcomes of a missional community	What are we trying to accomplish?
The principles of incarnational living	How are we to live?
The importance of serving the least of these with an outward focus	Who are we called to serve?
Discipleship	How will we become more like Jesus?
Group facilitation skills	How will we organize and manage the group dynamic?
The values and DNA of a missional community	What is important to us?
Gaining ownership and buy-in	How do we know if our people are on board?
The development and use of spiritual gifts	What can we expect from those who are part of our missional community?
Helping people reach their network of relationships	How can we help our people reach those in their natural sphere of influence?
Providing coaching and support	How can we be intentional about stretching and supporting those in our missional community?
Identifying apprentices and developing them as leaders	How can we find and develop more leaders?
Group multiplication	What is our plan as we grow?

Get going

As we form communities, we need to be action-oriented. It's easy to fall into just talking, but what's needed is a balance between processing ideas and taking action. So do something; make sure there's an action component to whatever you're talking about. Get started now, even if you don't have all of the pieces in place. Forward motion will help people act their way into a new way of thinking. Here are some strategies for getting started:

Start gathering together on a regular basis. During the group time, worship together, support one another, and encourage one another. Help one another stay on track with mission. Ask each other questions to help everyone stay on track with mission. Here are some good options:

> *Make it reproducible. As you get ready to start missional communities, adopt a reproducible model that others can readily imitate. As you answer these questions, keep the process simple so that it is easily passed on to others.*
> *– Dave*

- How have you experienced God this week?
- What are you hearing from him?
- In whom do you see God working?

Start a missional ministry of some kind. There's nothing like stories of faith in action to encourage others to join. If you meet resistance from some within the group, don't let that stop you. Decide on a way to serve sacrificially outside of the group and invite along anyone who wants to join. Others in the group can engage in different kinds of missional activities. There's no rule that everyone has to serve in the same way. Some may serve at the Salvation Army; others may tutor at the neighborhood school. There are hundreds of possibilities, and no one right answer.

Remind each other of God's involvement in your lives and ministries. At the end of the group I'm in, we gather in a circle to pray—holding hands, but facing outward. Our physical posture is a reminder that we are blessed in order to be a blessing to others. We are connected to one another, but serving the world around us.

Create groups-within-a-group. Depending on the size of your missional community, you may need to create smaller breakout groups where deeper and more personal sharing is possible. Groups of four to seven are optimal for holding one another accountable, and for providing more personalized support.

Make disciples. A missional community is a disciple-making community. This is where disciples are made. Members engage not only in their own personal transformation as growing disciples, but also in making new disciples. Create intentional ways for helping people reach out to those within their spheres of influence. Provide

> I love my kids. Because I love them, I talk about them a lot. And I pray for them a lot. When you meet, talk about the people you're reaching out to and pray for them. Share what's happening in their lives as they move closer to Jesus.
>
> – Dave

discipleship resources for those who are spiritually responsive. Decide on clear behaviors that indicate what a disciple is and does. Remember that discipleship is not purely a one-on-one activity; groups can disciple as well.

By getting started, a missional community becomes a closely knit group on mission together. As individuals engage their own personal transformation and the transformation of those they reach, the group will start seeing the signs of something bigger. They'll see spiritual transformation taking hold in the larger community around them.

A few years back in Ecuador, there was a small Quechua-speaking church in the slum community on the fringes of the city of Ambato, the fourth-largest city in the country. Many of the indigenous people in the mountains were no longer able to farm, so they migrated to the city. There they were second-class citizens, taking the most menial of jobs: carriers at the local market. They physically carried loads of goods around the city to the market. The small church on the fringes of the city was made up of these people. When they saw the reality of their community and the needs their own people were facing, they were faced with a choice. The church could shut their eyes to the needs, focusing only on spirituality and a future of heaven someday. Or, in the midst of their spirituality, they could engage the pain and problems of the community they found themselves in.

They chose the latter. The church decided to invest in one of their most promising young people and pooled their money to send him to school. When he finished his education, he helped lead the church into some community-engagement projects. Their first project was to create a little savings-and-loan association. They had just twelve members at the beginning, with each one contributing one dollar into the savings-and-loan chest.

The savings-and-loan association worked diligently to engage with the neighborhood. Money went toward community health projects, housing improvements, and small business loans. Some specific initiatives included classes to teach parents how to better care for their children, starting a daycare for children whose mothers had to work, and offering vocational training.

The operation, run through anon-governmental organization, was simple, transparent, and well-run. It grew from twelve members to 335. Their capital was $42,000, up from $12. The church grew as well, from twenty-plus people to 150, as they chose to engage holistically in the community around them—the very poor serving the very poor.

Stay with it

When we lead a missional community, we'll need to help those who are a part of it grow both spiritually and personally. Here are some ways to do that:

Challenge and stretch them. Have you ever noticed that we grow the most during times of difficulty or adversity? Most of us need challenges in order to grow. If you

> As soon as you have two missional community leaders, start meeting together as a learning community. Share personally with one another, and learn from one another. Encourage your leaders to start investing in the development of new leaders.
> — Dave

see someone on the fence about trying something new, encourage him or her to give it a try. Sometimes stepping up to the plate is the challenge people need to move to the next level of their development.

Support and encourage them. As people step out toward new challenges, they'll need a listening ear and a caring response. Provide ample encouragement, support, and prayer for those in your missional community. It will give them the stamina to keep traveling this often-difficult journey of missional ministry.

Provide coaching and peer gatherings. Give people the opportunity to gather with coaches, and with their peers, for intentional conversations. Ask these questions: What's working? What's not working? What needs to change? What are you learning? What's next?

Help people develop and use their spiritual gifts. Look for evidence of spiritual gifts, and point it out whenever you see it. Teach people in your missional community about spiritual gifts and how to identify them. Challenge them to use their gifts and to develop them further.

Encourage ongoing learning. Read books together that target the areas where you sense God is calling your group to grow. You may want to read about missional communities themselves, about discipleship, about sharing your faith, or any number of other topics. Keep the ideas and discussion flowing.

Keep growing

As you lead a missional community, or walk alongside those who do, where are you seeing God at work? How can you join God in what he's doing to see the formation and expansion of new missional communities? Below are several different ways to multiply missional communities:

You need to be selective. Many new workers are too eager to start more groups, and are given leadership roles too soon. If someone isn't making disciples, that person isn't yet ready to lead a group. Just because someone is eager to lead doesn't mean he or she's ready to lead.
– Dave

Develop new leaders. Look for people with the potential to become missional community leaders. Who do you see who's living fruitfully as a disciple? Who is effectively engaging culture? Consider college or seminary students, current small-group leaders, or disciplers. They may be ready to grow into missional community leaders. Invest where you see fruit to raise up new leaders for missional communities. Don't hesitate to partner new leaders together. People often lead more effectively in teams, especially when there's complementary giftedness.

Encourage existing leaders to identify apprentices. Suggest to those who have successfully formed missional communities that they begin developing and raising up other leaders. They can begin by looking for those who are fruitful in their personal ministries. When they've identified those people, current missional community leaders are in a unique position to engage in on-the-job training. They can model skills and behaviors, and provide direct feedback and assistance to their apprentices as they practice new skills. In many ways, current missional community leaders are in the best position to develop new leaders, through apprenticing.

Look to the newest disciples. Each new believer represents the seeds of a new missional community. Assume that every new follower of Jesus might be the beginning of a new faith community. With each new believer, we face the question of whether to fold them into our community or help them start their own. Let the default choice be to start a new one whenever possible. Help new believers reach their network of relationships, and find the person of peace who can form a new community around them.

Celebrate. If you've formed a missional community, take some time to celebrate. You've accomplished a lot. You've started a community of believers who gather together to experience authentic relationships, sacrificial service, and spiritual transformation.

Consider new journeys. God may be calling you on to other journeys. For many people, leading a missional community is a precursor to starting churches. For others, those journeys are synonymous. But whatever your beliefs on church structure, it's essential for fruitful missional community leaders to consider how they can expand their ministry beyond a single missional community. That could mean branching more into leadership development or coaching. It could mean starting new missional communities. It could mean starting a church, or a network of missional communities. Take some time to reflect on your successes, your learnings, and what you're hearing from God. What might he have for you next?

Imagine more and more missional communities being formed. Imagine those people developing authentic relationships, serving sacrificially, and seeing spiritual transformation in the world around them. Imagine the vast impact we would have.

Momentum like that will require leadership and organization. Who will lead all of these communities? How will they be supported and resourced? How will we organize all of these missional communities to be optimally effective and healthy? How will we link them together with one another? In short: How will we capitalize on the movement of the Holy Spirit when it happens?

We need to plan ahead for growth by developing our leadership structure. That's the subject of our next chapter.

Journey Guide: Forming communities

Checklist: You are here

engaging culture

forming communities/churches
- authentic relationships
- sacrificial service
- spiritual transformation
- gathering for worship and prayer
- gift-based ministry
- making more and better disciples

developing leadership

multiplying movements

Discussion questions: for you and your team

- What are you already doing?
- What's going well?
- What do you hear God saying to you?
- What reflections do you have on this chapter?

Guided prayer: for you and your team

Spend time as a team in visioning prayer. Ask the following questions,
allowing time for people to respond aloud in prayer:

- How can we form communities based on authentic relationships?
- How can we model sacrificial service through our communities?
- How can we worship God together?
- How can we serve as Jesus served?

End with prayer for spiritual transformation.

Action planning guide

"Forming missional communities" coaching questions:

- How are you developing authentic relationships?
- How are you engaging in sacrificial service?
- How are you fostering spiritual transformation?
- How are you gathering for worship and prayer?
- How are you encouraging gift-based ministry?
- How are you making more and better disciples?

Based on where you are in forming missional communities, work through the following questions and action steps together with your team:

 **Get ready**

Action points:

- Pray and respond to God's leading
- Clarify and model the basics:
    - o Authentic relationships
    - o Sacrificial service
    - o Spiritual transformation
- Identify a cause or service focus for your missional community
- Be ready to respond to anyone who wants to follow Jesus

Questions to discuss with your team:

- What are the essential ingredients of your missional community?
- What are the distinctives of your missional community?

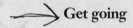 **Get going**

Action points:

- Meet together to form a missional community
- Share stories about Jesus and how he changed us
- Ask questions to facilitate learning
- Start rhythm of serving together sacrificially

Questions to discuss with your team:

- How will you incorporate the following elements into your gathering time?
    - o Authentic relationships
    - o Spiritual transformation
    - o Sacrificial service
- How will you include newcomers into your missional community?

⟶ Stay with it

Action points:

- Continue the disciple-making process together—keep teaching to obey
- Facilitate smaller groups as your missional community grows
- Identify potential missional community leaders
- Establish coaching relationships for every missional community leader
- Tell stories of how God is working
- Assume every new believer is the first member of a new missional community

Questions to discuss with your team:

- How have you seen God working in and through this missional community?
- How can you help people develop and use their spiritual gifts?

⟶ Keep growing

Action points:

- Stay focused
    - o Have faith conversations
    - o Help people along the path of faith
    - o Keep looking for persons of peace
- Expect every new follower of Jesus will start a new missional community
- Train everyone to focus on their relational networks (oikos)
- Celebrate the start of new missional communities
- Pray, pray, pray

Questions to discuss with your team:

- Where do you see opportunities to start new missional communities?
- What can you do to help prepare new missional community leaders?

Chapter 7

Developing leadership

A ny missional community—whether it's a house church, small group, or more traditional church—will require organizational sustainability in order to flourish. This means that even something organic—a movement of God—requires that we structure it in order to steward it well. Let's look at a well-known historical example.

John Wesley and George Whitfield were two very successful eighteenth-century evangelists; they both won thousands of converts as traveling circuit preachers. Yet Whitfield, at the end of his life said, "My converts are like a rope of sand." What a chilling statement. The converts didn't last. They didn't become disciples. On the other hand, Wesley left behind an entire movement of churches. During his lifetime, Wesley and his followers won 140,000 people to Christ. Yet in the generation after his death, countless thousands more came to know Christ; and today there are still people coming to faith who can trace their spiritual heritage back to the Wesley revival.

What was the difference between Whitfield and Wesley? The difference was a reproducible system. It was Wesley's critics who identified the secret. They called his followers Methodists—not as a compliment, but as a derogatory label. Yet they had accurately identified the secret: a simple, reproducible system (or method) which empowered ordinary people to do extraordinary things.

What precisely did Wesley do? So many thousands came to know Christ through his preaching that he had to form new groups and churches—

and he had to use new converts to lead them. He developed reproducible approaches that enabled them to function effectively as leaders while they learned. They grew into their leadership as they continued to serve, evangelize, make disciples, and raise up more leaders from the harvest. He established regional circuits that were made up of multiplying groups called societies, from which trained lay people provided pastoral care within a context of basic Christian community.

After creating the societies, Wesley felt the need to lower the bar even further. He founded an even smaller multiplying unit called class meetings—something we might call accountability and discipleship groups. Wesley viewed these class meetings as a means of evangelism. In spite of his legendary public preaching itinerary, he believed that it was in these groups that salvation was actually applied to the souls of converts. In fact, his circuit preachers were not to preach in a place where class meetings were not being formed. He told them, "Preach in as many places as you can. Start as many classes as you can. Do not preach without starting new classes." Preaching was merely a preamble, a means to awaken people to their need for Christ. It was within the relationship of a class meeting that they actually encountered Christ and began their relationship with him.

> Often I'm telling church planters not to start worship services until they've started making disciples first. Likewise, Jesus didn't train his disciples to start services to make disciples, but rather to make disciples to start churches. Consider gathering monthly after you've started three missional communities. This is a great time to celebrate together what God is doing. Consider meeting twice each month after four missional communities are gathering. Resist meeting weekly until at least five missional communities have begun.
> - Dave

What Wesley did was plan for the future, in order to get the most out of what God was doing. He thought ahead and organized to make sure that multiplication was happening at every level. By creating a system of leadership development, he retained a much larger share of the harvest than had he simply left his converts to their own devices after conversion.

Far from hindering the work of the Holy Spirit, a good organizational plan helps us make the most of the fruit the Holy Spirit grows. All life and growth, however natural, needs some structure to sustain it. God has built in biological structure at a cellular level, even among the simplest organisms. Living things don't always need a lot of structure, but some is necessary for life to thrive. Developing leadership for our ministries is no exception. If we want to have a healthy, functional pipeline of new leaders being developed, we need to put some type of system in place to support that. Otherwise even the most promising beginnings fizzle out.

Solid planning is essential for a sustained movement; the strategic groundwork for developing and supporting leaders must be laid. How can we organize and provide structure for what God is doing in order to give it the best chance of flourishing?

When creating a leadership structure for our ministry, we need to think about two primary areas: people development and organizational development. Wesley did both of these, and we'll be discussing both throughout the rest of this chapter.

Part 1: People development

People development is how you choose to go about developing individual ministry leaders. Regardless of what structure we choose, we need to develop leaders. But we're not talking about an institution here; we're talking about the people of God—a community on mission together. Because of the organic, relational, personal nature of the missional community, we need an equally relational means of leadership development—coaching.

Coaching is a relational way to develop leaders and organize local expressions of the church. We're still about authentic relationships, sacrificial service, and spiritual transformation as we make disciples. Coaching is simply a means to those ends. It helps us stay effectively on mission.

Coaching means coming alongside another person or team, to help them

> I was so blessed, when I started planting a church, to have Steve Ogne come alongside and coach me. His consistent presence throughout our journey was key to our effectiveness. Every leader needs a coach. As you focus on leadership development, make certain someone is coaching you—and that you're coaching leaders.
>
> — Dave

find out what God wants them to do and then help them to do it. Although the term coaching is relatively new in a ministry context, the practice is not. Coaching has been practiced in a variety of ways for thousands of years. Coaching has been known under the names of discipleship, leadership development, and pastoral training.

Coaches come alongside to help, just as Barnabas came alongside Paul, and then Paul came alongside Timothy and others. By encouraging and challenging, coaches empower others for ministry. Barnabas may never have been in the starring role, but without him many others would not have been able to accomplish the great things for God that they did. Through his investment in people, his impact was exponential.

John Wesley's circuit-riding preachers were, functionally speaking, ministry coaches. Whenever we see people intentionally come alongside others to help them in their life and ministry and help them listen to the Holy Spirit, there's coaching going on. People are not divided up neatly into sections labeled "ministry," "personal," "skills," or "dreams." Those qualities are all woven together in us and the seams are not clear.

> The more I coach leaders, the more important this point is to me. My job as a coach is to help leaders listen to the Holy Spirit and do as he says. How can I do that if I haven't learned to listen to the Spirit and do as he says in my own life? Coaches have to listen well to the Spirit; otherwise, we won't be able to help others listen well.
>
> — Dave

The goal of coaching is helping someone succeed. And what is success? It's finding out what God wants us to do and doing it. Given that definition, success will certainly look differently with different people, but all of it will be tied into accomplishing biblical mission. Far from a top-down program designed to accomplish preconceived ends, coaching empowers individual believers to listen to the Spirit and act in accordance with the mission they sense God calling them toward. Coaching relationships facilitate the process of listening to the Spirit and taking action accordingly.

Missional church leader Brandon Hatmaker told me about a coaching conversation he had that led to significant changes in his ministry:"I had an experience with Alan Graham, president and founder of Mobile Loaves and Fishes (www.mlfnow.org) who was coaching me through and teaching me to serve the homeless by starting with meeting immediate needs. The most profound moment came when he helped me see that empowering volunteers wasn't just to eradicate hunger on the streets of Austin, but to focus on the volunteers themselves as a part of their discipleship. Ephesians 4 came alive for me and completely restructured how we engaged service."

How does coaching work?

I've coached ministry leaders for pretty much forever now. When all is said and done, here's what needs to happen in each coaching session: prepare, engage, and act. This cycle is what makes coaching effective. It's what gets things done: preparing for the session in advance, interacting during the session, and then determining next steps at the end of the session.

When people come into the coaching session prepared with a clear idea of what they want to talk about, the conversation flows much more effectively and saves time. The coach can aid this process by preparing questions in advance for the person to think through, which allows them to come better prepared for the coaching conversation. Examples include: "Where are you seeing God at work?" "What needs to change?"

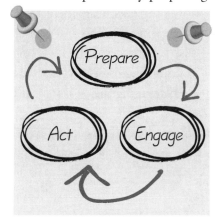

Helpful preparation questions include:
- *What insights have I had since our last session?*
- *What challenges and/or problems am I facing now?*
- *What opportunities are available to me right now?*
- *What do I want to focus on during my coaching session?*

– Dave

During the coaching session itself, the coach engages the person being coached through listening, and by asking more questions to help them think through their challenges and options, and to help plan a coherent course of action. As the session draws to a close, the coach and the ministry leader can determine the next steps to be taken... which, of course, informs the preparation for the next coaching conversation.

This simple cycle of prepare, engage, and act is what makes for effective coaching, supervision, and team leadership. It's what allows people to engage meaningfully and track on their progress in a simple way. I've created an online coaching log utilizing the prepare, engage, and act cycle, based on my many years of experience with it, at ***www.mycoachlog.com***. Coaches can use this system to help track leadership development in their ministry.

What makes coaching so powerful?

People are at least twice as fruitful when they're in coaching relationships. This includes coaching relationships that are focused on helping people live and lead missionally. Good coaching empowers people by:

- Providing encouragement for the journey
- Cultivating wisdom and strategic insights
- Discovering breakthrough opportunities
- Maintaining focus on the truly important
- Transforming vision into reality

Coaching is the core discipline for effective leadership development. It creates a pipeline of new leaders and new missional initiatives.

Potential applications include:

- Discipleship of new believers
- Personal and ministry development for emerging missional leaders
- Formation of new missional communities
- Starting and multiplying new ministry initiatives

Coaching is flexible enough to be helpful in a variety of ways, depending on the needs of the people involved. The most commonly known type of coaching is one-on-one—in other words, one person coaching and another receiving the coaching. This approach allows for total focus on the agenda of the one person being coached.

However, another extremely helpful type of coaching is what I call cluster coaching. That's one coach working with three people at the same time. This is particularly helpful if those three people share similar goals. For example, if I coach three missional leaders at once, for an hour and a half, I could give focused attention to each leader for half an hour, while the others listen and take away learnings from that time as well. This approach is usually time-saving, cost-effective, and has the added benefit of peer learning. I've been doing cluster coaching for a while now, and it works.

I've found it works best to coach either one-on-one or one-on-three. Coaching two people at a time can create the obstacle of comparison (one is doing better than the other); however, I've found that coaching three creates a supportive community. I've seen how people enjoy journeying alongside others,

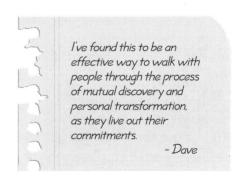

I've found this to be an effective way to walk with people through the process of mutual discovery and personal transformation, as they live out their commitments.
— *Dave*

learning from people in similar situations, and sharing common obstacles and solutions. There's a great deal we can learn from one another, and that element can make cluster coaching even more valuable than individual coaching.

Whatever form it takes, coaching is central to how we develop new leaders to sustain missional ministry. Dave DeVries uses an approach that he calls a coaching cohort. It focuses on one facet of the disciple-making process—for example, engaging culture. The coach facilitates the discussion, everyone contributes to the learning process, and the time concludes with each person making an individualized commitment to move forward.

Best of all, coaching is easily reproducible. Once we've experienced having someone who listens, guides, and asks the questions no one else asks, we long to offer it to others. That kind of relational connection is like gold too precious to hoard. We are compelled to give it away, investing in others as we ourselves have been invested in.

Part 2: Organizational development

People development and organizational development are linked: As you coach and develop more leaders, the organization also grows. This reality often creates challenges for leaders; they quickly find that what they've been doing successfully suddenly doesn't work anymore. The senior leader who's been developing other leaders himself or herself now begins running short of time. He or she is no longer able to develop as many leaders as are needed for a growing organization.

What works at one stage won't work at the next stage. We need to continue reorganizing as we move from one developmental stage to the next.

Organizational development simply refers to how we choose to structure and grow our organization as a whole. First of all, what is the organizing principle? This will help

> One of the shifts I made as a church planter was from developing volunteers to developing leaders. As I began developing leaders, they were able to develop volunteers, and their numbers multiplied.
>
> Then I had to shift from developing leaders to raising up leaders of leaders. This moved me to a new level of leadership and required that we expand our structure.
>
> As I focused on leaders who developed leaders, the breadth of our ministry expanded. It began slowly at first, but then accelerated as our leaders raised up more leaders.
>
> - Dave

you create a picture of what the ministry will look like as it grows. If you have a network of house churches that's organized by all the members coming together once a month for worship, that will look different than if you have a network of leaders of house churches where only the leaders come together once a month for support and development.

As you think through how to organize your ministry, consider the people flow. How do people come to faith? How do they get engaged in missional ministry? How do they get involved in community? In what environments will people gather together? If you have public worship, how do you engage visitors? Can you draw a picture of how all the pieces fit together?

What makes a good missional coach?

1. *Principle-based perspective:* Thorough understanding of the basic principles that undergird incarnational missional ministry

2. *Credibility and connection:* The ability to connect helpfully and relationally with missional leaders

3. *Creative contextualization:* A capacity for outside-the-box thinking about what kind of approaches will work in a particular context

4. *Sustainable organization:* The ability to help leaders develop and adapt sustainable systems as their missional ministry grows

5. *Multiplication outlook:* Focuses on the reproducible nature of missional living

If you want to see more, check out Appendix E

If you're a church planter, this is the time when you need to work on the church rather than in the church. Take a step back to see how all of the pieces fit together—or aren't fitting together. How can you help those on your team understand how their piece fits into the rest of the puzzle? All of this will give you some important clues about how to organize as your ministry grows.

Whatever we want to end up with, we must start with in seed form. We need to always ask ourselves the question, "What if this works?" If this new ministry takes off and grows, how will we handle the growth? What will we need to multiply? Group leaders? Meeting space? Discipler/mentors? Teachers? How will we do that?

By creating a growth plan *before* the growth takes place, you'll be ready. As you expand, you develop people. As you develop more people, the organization needs to adjust and expand to accommodate continued growth. Perhaps counter intuitively: As God is blessing, problems arise. Remember Acts 6 with the feeding of the widows in the early church? Health and growth led to leadership overload. People started getting missed. The leadership required reorganization to sustain growth at the same level of quality. And as a result of that reorganization, the church grew even more.

Contemporary churches often hit the same types of road bumps in their organizational growth. When I was first planting a church, I found that I was getting tired and discouraged every few weeks. I prayed the psalms, crying out to God, asking for his help, praying for perspective. I was on the lookout for unconfessed sin. I tried counting my blessings. Nothing. I wasn't getting anywhere.

Then the thought came, "Why don't you sit down and draw an organizational chart of the church?" My first response was one of irritation. "An org chart? Hmm…well, since God isn't answering my prayers, I might as well do that." I wrote my name down at the top, drew the chart, and discovered that I had 27 direct reports. That's 27 lines going to my name with arrows. I threw my pen down on the paper and thought, "No wonder I'm tired! I don't have a spiritual problem here. I have a Moses problem. I'm trying to do too much stuff myself." (See Exodus 18:13–27 for more on the "Moses problem.") My church had grown to the point that reorganization was required.

For me, that meant changing my leadership style. I had to shift from doing much of the ministry myself into an equipping role. It's like driving a stick shift—you have to shift gears to avoid stalling out. Staying in the same gear—when a different one is required for the

As a leader, it's important to understand your leadership capacity. Trying to personally do more than you're capable of doing will ultimately decrease your effectiveness. Investing more time in leadership development will actually increase effectiveness and decrease the burden you may be carrying as a leader.

— Dave

conditions—will lead to ineffectiveness. Gear-shifting is essential for going on to the next phase.

When something is working, we can ask, "How can we do even more?" When something is not working, we need to either change it or drop it. As Jim Herrington, network leader and founder of Mission Houston, said, "How can we further intentionalize our efforts, in order to accelerate our results?" That's a great coaching question that leads to positive change.

We need to know what we're measuring. What constitutes success? Jesus told us to make disciples. So what we measure needs to be an indicator of how disciples live, what they do, etc. We need to regularly reevaluate our organization to determine if it is still functioning in the best way to accomplish the intended purpose.

Build in regular reevaluation time to ask questions like these:

1. What are we trying to accomplish? How will we measure that?
2. In what ways does each ministry and system connect, in order to accomplish our goals?
3. How well do people understand the ministry flow—i.e., how we carry out ministry?
4. How are people involved in the process of shaping and fulfilling goals?
5. In what ways does the organizational structure facilitate ministry? In what ways does it hinder ministry from being accomplished?

Consider management, leadership, communications, and systems. By setting aside regular time for an organizational checkup, we create a planning cycle where we take the ideas generated by one evaluation, build them into the system, then check to see how it's working. The criteria of whether something is working or not always comes down to whether we're accomplishing the intended purpose. What are we trying to produce? What are we measuring? How is it measuring up?

Whatever we measure is what we hope to multiply. And whenever we see multiplication, we need to move into the next cycle of measuring, planning, and restructuring—because what worked in the last phase of development may not work in the next one.

Restructuring the system

When you have a system that is multiplying disciples, groups, leaders or churches, it's common to see a slowing of momentum at the third of fourth generation. One solution is to intentionally move a stronger leader out from the center of the system to the edges, so that you can see stronger multiplication coming from that point.

In an electricity distribution network, a central node is established in order to distribute energy. When the line gets weak, a new node can be established to extend energy from that point. In the same way, putting a stronger leader out on the fringes creates a new center of energy that can extend a system even further.

When problems are caused by growth, recognize it for the opportunity that it is. This is your chance to reorganize and expand with the growth, rather than letting it overwhelm you and burn out your leaders. Use a system of coaching that will distribute and empower a broader leadership structure, so that your ministry will continue to flourish.

So, how do you do that?

Get ready

Who is coaching you? You can talk all you want about the value of coaching, but if you don't have a coach, your actions will speak louder than your words. I've been coaching church planters for a network leader who refuses to have a coach himself. While he says coaching is important, he's sending the message that it's optional.

– Dave

The early stages of setting up coaching as a tool for leadership development are the most critical. The good news is that if you take the time on the front end to put the essentials in place, your coaching system can run smoothly, just under the surface of your ministry. Getting ready includes casting vision, picking the right people, and providing quality orientation.

As with most areas of ministry, casting vision is essential. Those in ministry will need to understand that coaching is good. It's a relational investment. It means you believe in them, and their potential. It does not mean they're behind and need a special tutor; it is a leadership development track. Of course, if we're to have any credibility whatsoever, they'll need to know that we have coaches too. That's the ultimate statement of value.

When the vision is cast, we'll need to select the right people to serve as coaches. These people may or may not have any prior training in coaching or in ministry, but that's okay. We want to select based on each person's heart, God-given gifts, and obedience in discipleship. We can provide training—we can't provide heart. So what qualities do we need to look for in our coaches? We look for people who:

- Empower and develop others
- Listen well, and ask insightful questions
- Encourage and care for others
- Think clearly and strategically
- Continue to learn and grow personally

We'll also need to select the right people to invest in. Look for those who are already fruitful in the earlier journeys: engaging culture and forming missional communities. These are the people who can introduce us to their friends, their disciples, and their communities. They are already living missionally, and God is blessing their ministries. We already know their character, and we've seen them under stress.

These two groups—potential leaders and potential coaches—are the two groups we need to be investing in. If we're working in an all-volunteer setting, we'll need at least one coach for every three missional leaders. We will need to invest time, training, and resourcing in these people. That said, training can often be done with both coaches and leaders, since the majority of people in missional ministry are a little bit of both. Our orientation can include both coach training and leadership skill training.

Consider including some of the following missional leadership topics in your coach training:

- definitions of a missional community
- functions and outcomes of a missional community (i.e., What are you trying to accomplish?)
- how we structure and support our missional communities
- the seven principles of incarnational living (see Chapter 2)
- the importance of an outward focus and serving the "least of these"
- promoting disciplemaking and discipleship in your missional communities
- group facilitation skills
- the values and DNA of our missional communities
- gaining ownership and buy-in
- promoting the use of spiritual gifts
- helping people reach their network of relationships
- identifying apprentices and developing them as leaders
- providing coaching and support for leaders
- group multiplication strategies

As your leadership development system becomes more complex, and your options multiply, you may want to consider getting a coach specifically to help you design and implement an effective strategy. Although you could certainly take much of this material and run with it, I've found that you can double or even triple your effectiveness by working with a coach.

Once we've given our people some things to think about in the orientation, the only way they'll really learn is through practice. It's time to get started—both coaching and leading. It's time to connect our leaders and our coaches and start meeting.

I was coaching one leader, and we began to focus on clarifying his ministry objectives for the coming year. As I asked him about what had given him a sense of accomplishment in the past, he realized that it had been mentoring younger leaders. This time of reflection helped him frame his objectives for the new year in a way that included mentoring as a priority. Reflecting on his previous actions led him to determine appropriate further actions to take as he moved forward.

- Dave

Get going

As coaches and leaders begin working together, they'll engage in an action-reflection-action cycle. After leaders have engaged in ministry, they can take some time with their coaches to reflect, taking stock of where they're at and dreaming about where they want to be. Coaches can help leaders get clarity on their next step. After taking that next step, they can engage in reflection again.

Instead of trying (unsuccessfully) to see every step of the way, just work on discerning the next step. Pray and listen to the Holy Spirit, allowing him to guide the process as you focus on the destination. Then leaders can act in obedience to what they're hearing alongside their coach. After acting, re-engage in reflection to identify the step after that.

Something within us needs to dream, even when the reality is far down the road. But there are things we can do, decisions we can make, actions we can take. Many of those actions may be small things, but when put together many small things can add up to real change.

Stay with it

As leaders and coaches are getting out there coaching and leading, they'll need to both stretch and support—the rubber bands and shoelaces mentioned in Chapter 5. Regular peer gatherings with other leaders and coaches will help tie them together. These are times to connect, relate, share what's been going on in our ministries, and hear what's been going on in the ministries of others. The number of ideas people get from peer gatherings is astronomical—and it's all done without teaching. Just hearing from others about what's working and what's not working facilitates learning, while prayer and encouragement cements the support.

Leaders need coaches to help them grow in their leadership skills. Coaches need coach-mentors to help them develop in their coaching competency. As you develop your leadership pathway, continue to raise up leaders, coaches, and coach-mentors for ongoing effectiveness.

- Dave

As people grow into their roles as leaders and coaches, they'll also need to continue stretching and growing. Coaches can take targeted assessments, which can help them focus on the specific skills or competency areas they need to grow in. Armed with this information, they can work together with their coach-mentors to continue developing their coaching skills. Likewise, leaders can work with their coaches to create personal development plans highlighting the areas where they need to grow. Ongoing reading, assessment, and practice—all under the umbrella of coaching—will keep them on track.

This is also an opportunity for proactive restructuring of the organization. Leaders need to decide how to structure their ministry for optimal effectiveness and sustainability. There are many, many different ways that this can look and the right choice is largely dependent on ministry context. Leaders can make use of their coaching relationships to help think through their vision, philosophy, and/or model of ministry, and receive valuable feedback in return.

Keep growing

Assuming that the previous journeys of engaging culture and forming missional communities are increasingly becoming a part of the genetic code of your ministry, you'll likely see some new leaders whom God is unmistakably blessing. Help these leaders organize for sustainability— and help them learn to develop new leaders and new coaches out of those they're reaching. This is where broader-scope reproducibility and multiplication really take root.

Youth for Christ (YFC) has seen many new leaders come out of those they've served through compassion ministries. In a predominantly Islamic nation in Asia, YFC developed a ministry to young homeless children from the streets of the city. These young people, who have no family and little hope for a future, are cared for and become members of small group homes with house parents. They are loved, fed, clothed and introduced to the teachings of Jesus. They are enrolled at public and private schools, helped with tutoring, and begin to be formally educated for the first time in their lives. The fact that they go to local schools, rather than an independent

Christian school, means that they begin to be Kingdom people early, sharing the Kingdom with their classmates. The project has been going for many years and YFC is now seeing those who arrived as children find Christ, show leadership, and make their way to university and beyond.
In Antsirabe, a town in the central highlands of Madagascar, YFC began offering English classes to children, in response to a request from a child. The boy brought his friends; they used the Bible as a basic text for their learning, and each week the numbers of students grew. This little work has now become a major ministry within Antsirabe. Hundreds of young people attend classes each week. The local government schools have backed the venture, providing their facilities and resources to be used by YFC workers on the weekends for free. An astonishing outcome has been that most of the current YFC staff are ex-students of this ministry.

The new communities and new leaders that God raises up require new tools and resources to keep them replicating. We can't be fooled into funneling our resources into buildings or providing in-house goods and services for Christians. If we want to be good stewards and see a return on our investment, leadership development is where we need to be investing our resources: "Still other seed fell on good soil, where it produced a crop—a hundred, sixty or thirty times what was sown" (Matt. 13:8). When we see leaders whom God is blessing, we need to make sure their coaches are asking questions that really help them maximize their potential, such as:

- What successes have you had?
- How can you be intentional about moving your ministry toward multiplication?
- Who are some other missional leaders you could develop?
- What are you hearing from God?
- What are you sensing he has for you next?

As new missional communities, new ministries, and even new churches are replicating, some leaders—through prayer and the guidance of the Holy Spirit—may embark on the journey of multiplying movements.
SOMA Communities in Tacoma, Washington does a great job of developing its leaders relationally. New leaders are drawn from within

the community groups, where people can directly observe what existing leaders are doing. They see leaders opening up their homes, giving of their time and energy. They understand from the outset that being a leader in ministry isn't just an event—it takes your whole life. Because the leadership emphasis is at the grassroots level and focused on reproduction of smaller communities, SOMA is able to develop "average" people to be able to lead. They don't need to be superstars—they just need to have a relational connection and a willingness to serve.

The fundamental need for both people development and organizational development is coaching. Coaching is the central thread—the piece that holds all the rest of what we do together. If we want our ministry to reach its full potential, we need to develop and organize our leaders through coaching. Without coaching, missional leadership development simply doesn't work. It becomes institutional—rooted in meetings and training events—rather than relational.

> When you fully grasp how vital coaching is to the multiplication of leaders and groups, your effort to provide coaches for every leader will take a higher priority. Remember, you don't have to coach every leader, but you do need to provide a trained coach to come alongside every leader.
>
> - Dave

Leadership in the body of Christ is not about commanding, but about serving and equipping. It's about making someone else greater than ourselves. Jesus said, *"You know that the rulers of the Gentiles lord it over them, and their high officials exercise authority over them. Not so with you. Instead, whoever wants to become great among you must be your servant"* (Matt. 20:25-26).

Leadership in the body of Christ is about releasing others for ministry. In scripture we see a constant training and sending out of leaders to reach new people, form new communities, and develop more leaders. That's the pattern. Without a vast network of developing leaders, we cannot hope to live out the vast mandate Jesus left us with: to make disciples. So together, we develop new leaders—not in isolation, but in the context of community:

So Christ himself gave the apostles, the prophets, the evangelists, the pastors and teachers, to equip his people for works of service, so that the body of Christ may be built up until we all reach unity in the faith and in the knowledge of the Son of God and become mature, attaining to the whole measure of the fullness of Christ (Eph. 4:11-13).

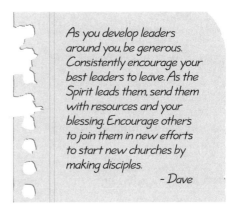

As you develop leaders around you, be generous. Consistently encourage your best leaders to leave. As the Spirit leads them, send them with resources and your blessing. Encourage others to join them in new efforts to start new churches by making disciples.

- Dave

If we're willing to provide the consistent investment of time and energy required to come alongside leaders to help them grow, the return on that investment will be phenomenal. Like compounding interest, our efforts will have a multiplying effect that makes a difference well beyond the walls of the church.

Journey Guide: Developing leadership

Checklist: You are here

engaging culture

forming communities/churches

developing leadership
- mobilizing
- apprenticing (show-how training)
- coaching
- leadership communities
- celebrating successes and learning from experiences
- affirming vision and values
- organizing for further expansion

multiplying movements

Discussion questions: for you and your team

- What are you already doing?
- What's going well?
- What do you hear God saying to you?
- What reflections do you have on this chapter?

Guided prayer: for you and your team

Leadership development is for everyone. Everyone should be being developed and everyone should be engaged in developing someone else. Ask each person to pray through the following questions:

- Who should I be investing in?
- What needs to be developed in them?
- How might I help them develop?

End by inviting the Holy Spirit to lead the process.

Action planning guide

"Developing leadership" coaching questions:

- How are you mobilizing leaders?
- How are you apprenticing leaders?
- How are you coaching leaders?
- How are you forming leadership communities?
- How are you celebrating successes and learning from experiences?
- How are you affirming vision and values?
- How are you organizing for further expansion?

Based on where you are in developing leadership, work through the following questions and action steps together with your team:

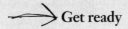 **Get ready**

Action points:

- Consider how Jesus developed leaders
- Recognize that without coaching, missional leadership simply doesn't work
- Orient new leaders
- Whatever we want to end up with, we start with in seed form
- Mold your model to fit your DNA, not vice-versa

Questions to discuss with your team:

- What will our organizing principles be?
- What unit will we measure to track growth?

Get going

Action points:

- Send new leaders out
- Cast vision for every leader having a coach
- Clarify tangible leadership outcomes
- Create opportunities for apprenticing and show-how training
- Rely on Holy Spirit to guide through listening and prayer

Questions to discuss with your team:

- In what environments will people gather together?
- What does our ministry flow chart look like? (i.e., How will people get involved?)

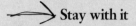 **Stay with it**

Action points:

- Form leadership communities
- Resource your leaders
- Assess and challenge your leaders
- Together coaches and leaders do the action-reflection-action cycle
- Coaches meet with mentor-coaches for ongoing skill development
- Continue to coach and develop new leaders

Questions to discuss with your team:

- Which people need to be networked together?
- What emerging leaders and coaches can you identify?

Keep growing

Action points:

- Multiply more leaders
- Invest in the coaching of every new leader
- Develop more coaches
- Provide ongoing training and support for new coaches
- Listen to the leading of the Holy Spirit
- Release proven multipliers to embark on the journey of multiplying movements

Questions to discuss with your team:

- What if it works?
- How will our leadership structure need to change as we grow?

Chapter 8

Multiplying movements

Something really important happens in Acts 13: We see Barnabas and Paul officially commissioned to go and start new communities of Jesus followers. This is where we see the early church move from starting new churches accidentally to starting new churches intentionally. Did churches exist before this point? Certainly. But they came about as a natural by-product of people following Jesus. Here is where the church became intentional about the process, and—not coincidentally—here is where the growth and multiplication of the church really took off.

From this point on, we can trace the ministry of Paul as he, along with various companions, not only plant new churches but multiply them, raising up new leaders as they go. They preached the gospel in Derbe, Lystra, Iconium, and Philippi, and raised up leaders such as Timothy and Lydia, then moved on to Thessalonica, Berea, Corinth, and Ephesus (Acts 16–18). Almost every place Paul and his companions went, they planted new churches.

Eventually Paul worked out of a home base in Ephesus at the school of Tyrannus (Acts 19:8–10), training leaders who then went out to reach the whole region of Asia Minor: "This went on for two years, so that all the Jews and Greeks who lived in the province of Asia heard the word of the Lord" (Acts 19:10). Most of the letters Paul wrote in the New Testament provide guidance to these fledgling churches he had planted and left in the hands of others, and some to churches he had never seen in person, planted by those he trained in Ephesus. (For a great treatment of the transformation of the Apostle Paul's leadership style over time, see Neil Cole's *Journeys to Significance*.)

We need to continue to move from accidental to intentional church planting today. Many of our churches are planted accidentally, whether from church splits, diverging visions, or people just not getting along. How much greater would the "return on investment" be if we became more intentional about starting new disciple-making communities—and even new movements?

Forming missional communities—and even developing strong leadership for those communities—doesn't end the journey. We need to see whole movements of churches worldwide reaching the whole range of communities out there. If we want to see spiritual transformation at every level—individual, group, societal, and worldwide—this is the journey that finally gets us there.

Where do we start? In this chapter on multiplying movements we'll address three questions:
• Where do we start?
• Who do we start with?
• How do we move forward?

Where do we start?

We start where Jesus left off—in Acts 1:8 just before his ascension: *"But you will receive power when the Holy Spirit comes on you; and you will be my witnesses in Jerusalem, and in all Judea and Samaria, and to the ends of the earth."*

The goal has never been just to start one church or one missional community. The goal is to reach all people with the transforming

> *The multiplication of churches is built on the making of disciples and the forming of missional communities. The more you focus on making disciples who make disciples, and the more missional communities that are formed, the more churches you'll see started.*
> *- Dave*

message of the gospel. Accomplishing that requires way more than one church or ministry—it requires multiplying movements. It also requires the crossing of bridges and barriers: language, cultural, social, economic, racial, etc.

Although we are sent to all people groups, near and far, our starting point is wherever we are right now—our own local Jerusalem. Our Jerusalem includes the people who live where we do and who are culturally similar to us. From there, we spread throughout our region: Judea and Samaria. At this point we begin to be stretched a bit. These are all people who live somewhat near us, but some of them are culturally different from us. Judeans, sure— but Samarians? Think of where you live. Who is in your Jerusalem? your Judea? your Samaria?

The next step from there takes us across massive cultural divides: the ends of the earth. That literally means all people groups. Jesus called us to be his witnesses, locally, regionally, and globally. We start where we are, but we don't stop there. We are to spread the message of the gospel to the ends of the earth.

Crossing those barriers will require the development of new apostolic and prophetic leaders who represent those groups. If we are starting a ministry within a group that is not our own, we need to start with an exit in mind. We'll need to empower someone else to lead after we're gone. Cross-cultural missionaries need to see their task as a midwife. The role is not to stay and pastor the church but to phase out once it is established. Taking this approach means that training and empowering local leadership needs to be a primary objective.

When we do go into another culture, we need to go in as learners and as listeners. In the era of colonialism, many missionaries went in with a paternalistic attitude ("I know better than you do and I'll help you improve"). That's a mistake we do not want to repeat today. Instead, we need to listen to the community leaders who are already there. We need to hear their stories, understand their values, and find out what matters to them.

Instead of counting how many people are part of your church, focus on how many people in your area are not part of any church. As you start new missional communities throughout your town or city, pray that the number of people outside the kingdom of God is decreasing. Consider how you can do your part to see the unreached people near you reached.

- Dave

- How do they adopt new ideas?
- How do leaders emerge?
- What are the qualifying characteristics of leaders?
- How are decisions made?
- What needs are their present beliefs filling?
- What needs are not being met?
- What has their past experience been with Christianity?

Healthy churches grow and reproduce other churches in their own culture and beyond. Community Christian Church in Chicago has multiplied to twelve locations in the Chicago area. That's an example of regional multiplication. The next step is global multiplication. Hope Chapel started in Hermosa Beach, California. They are now in Hawaii, Japan, and many other places because they were able to raise up apostolic leaders cross-culturally.

When we start churches cross-culturally, our task is not complete until these new churches are also participating in ministry multiplication. In this way we spread the transformative message of the gospel from Judea to Samaria to the ends of the earth.

Who do we start with?

We start with the proven leaders who are showing fruitfulness in their previous journeys. Ralph Moore, founder of the aforementioned Hope Chapel, was able to launch a multiplying movement in part because of his empowerment of proven leaders. He identified missional community leaders who could evangelize, disciple, and raise up other leaders. The leadership then prayed over these leaders, asking which ones God might be calling to become planters. Those who received confirmation engaged in an intensive equipping process in which they gathered a team and launched a new faith community.

The leaders who are engaging culture, forming missional communities, and developing other leaders are the ones we need to empower for multiplying movements. One of the most helpful ways to think about the different types of proven leaders is through the spiritual gifts: "It was he who gave some to be apostles, some to be prophets, some to be evangelists, and some to be pastors and teachers" (Eph. 4:11). Below are descriptions for the five different types of leadership gifting, also known as APEST, popularized by Alan Hirsch in his book The Forgotten Ways. The definitions for these roles are a composite drawn from that book, as well as from *Beyond Church Planting* by Robert E. Logan and Neil Cole. (Hirsch expands further on these roles in his latest book *The Permanent Revolution*.):

One important qualification to evaluate is whether a particular leader is a proven multiplier. The strength and influence of missional leaders is wholly dependent on their commitment to disciplemaking. Producing transformed lives, and seeing those lives reproduced in others, is a high value of missional leadership.
- Dave

1. **Apostle:** One sent to lay a foundation for the expansion of the church with a specific, God-given assignment. Apostles extend the gospel. As the "sent ones," they ensure that the faith is transmitted from one context to another and from one generation to the next. They are always thinking about the future, bridging barriers, establishing the church in new contexts, developing leaders, networking trans-locally. Yet if they focus solely on initiating new ideas and rapid expansion, they can leave people and organizations wounded. Shepherding and teaching functions are needed to ensure that people are cared for, rather than simply used.

2. **Prophet:** One who hears and speaks a specific word from God to a distinct person or persons. Prophets know God's will. They are particularly attuned to God and his truth for today. They bring correction and challenge the dominant assumptions we inherit from the culture. They insist that the community obey what God has commanded. They question the status quo. Without the other types of leaders in place, however, prophets can become belligerent activists or, paradoxically, disengage from the imperfection of reality and become "other-worldly."

3. **Evangelist:** One who is called to passionately seek out opportunities to share the gospel with others and lead them toward acceptance of Jesus.

Evangelists recruit. These infectious communicators of the gospel message recruit others to the cause. They call for a personal response to God's redemption in Christ, and also draw believers to engage the wider mission, growing the church. On the down side, evangelists can be so focused on reaching those outside the church that maturing and strengthening those inside is neglected.

4. **Shepherd:** One who has an overwhelming concern for the continuing care of a specific community. Shepherds nurture and protect. As caregivers of the community, they focus on the protection and spiritual maturity of God's flock, cultivating a loving and spiritually mature network of relationships, making and developing disciples. Shepherds value stability—sometimes to the detriment of the mission. They may also foster an unhealthy dependence between the church and themselves.

5. **Teacher:** One responsible for progressive growth in understanding and application of the truth. Teachers understand and explain. Communicators of God's truth and wisdom, they help others remain biblically grounded so they better discern God's will, guide others toward wisdom, help the community remain faithful to Christ's word, and construct a transferable doctrine. Without the input of the other functions, teachers can fall into dogmatism or dry intellectualism. They may fail to see the personal or missional aspects of the church's ministry.

Those who are curious about their own leadership leanings can take the APEST online self-assessment inventory, at **www.theforgottenways.org/apest.**

These five gifts form a continuum, and each type of leader will go about leading ministries differently. Generally speaking, leaders who fall along the side of apostle/prophet are better suited for a "start-and-go" approach. Apostles and prophets go into a new situation, start a ministry from scratch, raise up people who can take up leadership of the new church, and then move on to the next place. These are the people to start with for leading a movement.

At the same time, those who lean toward the shepherd/teacher end of the spectrum—"stay and grow"—will be needed as leaders of the local expression of the church. When those with evangelist, shepherd, or teacher gifts start a church, they also usually stay on as leaders.

All roles are necessary for a movement to cross cultural lines. For further context, look again at Ephesians 4:11, as well as the verses immediately following it:

> *So Christ himself gave the apostles, the prophets, the evangelists, the pastors and teachers, to equip his people for works of service, so that the body of Christ may be built up until we all reach unity in the faith and in the knowledge of the Son of God and become mature, attaining to the whole measure of the fullness of Christ (Eph. 4:11–13).*

The critical issue for maturity in the fullness of Christ is to raise up all five of these types of leaders from among the indigenous groups being reached. Apostolic leaders don't always have cross-cultural gifts—some work best within their own groups. Peter was called as an apostle to the Jews, the group he was a part of; whereas Paul was called as an apostle to the Gentiles, indicating a cross-cultural gifting.

Multiplication needs to happen in both arenas, within a culture and between cultures, but the strategy usually differs. Within a similar culture and a similar setting, church multiplication can occur by replicating what has already been proven to work. This is a franchise approach, and many successful multi-site churches are built on this approach, and healthy churches will continue to multiply at least within their own setting. Yet when reaching across cultures, additional experimentation is needed. The old formulas will likely not work in the new settings.

As Dr. D.T. Niles of Sri Lanka put it, "The gospel is like a seed, and you have to sow it…. Now, when missionaries came to our lands they brought not only the seed of the gospel, but their own plant of Christianity, flower pot included! So, what we have to do is to break the flowerpot, take out the seed of the gospel, sow it in our own cultural soil, and let our own version of Christianity grow."

How do we move forward?

Take the time to ask God, "What's our part in reaching the world beyond us?" Then, as you listen to the guidance of the Spirit, join in what he is doing.

— Dave

Crossing cultures, inventing new approaches and new structures for church… that's a big vision. How do we begin to move forward into it? So far we've identified our own Jerusalem, Judea, and Samaria—this gives us a picture of the mosaic that exists in our local sphere. It will take all kinds of missional communities to reach every segment of society, even within our region. Yet Jesus told us to be witnesses everywhere, to the ends of the earth. How?

We can't do everything, but we can focus on something. My most recent church plant has adopted the northwest corner of Madagascar as its ends-of-the-earth focus. If the church is to reflect the mosaic of different people in the world, our churches will need to take the initiative to reach out to different people groups. Even if your church is focusing most of its energy at the local "Jerusalem level," consider your ends-of-the-earth impact as well.

Here's where we also need to pray for workers to reach into those harvest fields. The harvest is plentiful but the workers are few. How can we contribute workers? We can develop leaders, and encourage them to examine their cross-cultural giftedness potential as well as their apostolic potential. If we are regularly engaged in a process of spotting, cultivating, empowering, and releasing leaders, some of those leaders may turn out to be cross-culturally gifted.

We can also contribute by multiplying our compassion ministries. Those can often branch across cultural and geographic lines. Partnering with existing nonprofits, or creating both internal and external ministries of the local church, are two different options. Networking the church in together with compassion ministries significantly impacts your outreach potential.

Getting a roadmap

Although each culture and context is different, and details will need to be worked out between apostolic leaders and their coaches, it's still helpful to have a basic roadmap. What follows is an overview of the last of our four journeys—the journey of multiplying movements. With this basic structure in hand, we'll at least have the right questions to ask as we work toward multiplying Kingdom ministry.

The assumed foundation for a multiplication movement is found in the three previous journeys: engaging culture, forming missional communities, and developing leadership. Those elements need to be in place first. If they are, this is where we can move from micro to macro—creating a self-sustaining, multiplying movement of Jesus-followers that has a lasting, long-term impact on the world around us. This is where things get really exciting. This is the shift from accidental to intentional.

Get ready

If you're at the point of embarking on a multiplying movement, you're already seeing some evidence of the Holy Spirit at work in your ministry. So at this point, the most important activities for setting your movement on the right track are to pray, plan, and identify leaders.

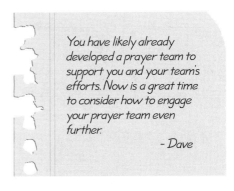

You have likely already developed a prayer team to support you and your team's efforts. Now is a great time to consider how to engage your prayer team even further.

- Dave

Although many people consider them near-opposites, prayer and planning actually go hand in hand. As we pray, we discern the heart of God and begin clarifying a vision of what this movement could look like. As that vision takes shape, we'll become aware of what type of structures we need to support it. How will the different units function? How will their leaders interact with each other? How will resourcing be provided? By asking the right questions, we'll be able to discern a structure and a plan that is best positioned to help the movement thrive and grow—and know how to best pray for this growing movement.

Get going

We need apostolic leaders. They are the ones who lead a movement. However, apostolic leaders are generally recognized after the fact, which leaves us with somewhat of a dilemma: How do we find these people and support them, when we don't know for sure who they are until they're already helping lead a movement?

Train every believer to become a trainer. Ying Kai makes this a priority in his ministry in Southeast Asia. For many years he was starting a new church every year. Then one day, while he was praying, God asked him, "What is better than planting churches?" God then answered the question for him: "training others to plant churches." Then God asked him, "Do you know what is better than training others to plant churches?" Again God answered the question for him: "training others to train others to plant churches." The result of this prayer is a church-planting movement that has now baptized more than one million believers.
— Dave

For a good example of this difficulty, re-read the history of the Apostle Paul. When he was holding coats during the stoning of Stephen, he probably didn't look like much of a candidate for apostolic leadership. When he was hunting down Christians and dragging them from their homes, even less so. Far from supporting him, the existing church leadership feared him greatly. Even after his conversion, they refused to meet with him for fear of a trap.

He needed a Barnabas. A Barnabas is someone who sponsors new leaders. If we are going to successfully foster multiplying movements, we need to function as a Barnabas, looking for new leaders to sponsor. We never know who the next apostle Paul will be, so we need to treat every new believer as if he or she might be that next apostolic leader. Look especially for those who are able and willing to cross cultural lines, spreading the gospel into different geographical areas or different segments of society. Bicultural and bilingual leaders are especially effective.

Humberto Del Arca is a Barnabas. He is helping lead a multiplying movement of more than two hundred churches in Honduras, and has a heart for spreading that movement across cultures. Toward that end, he keeps his eyes open for cross-cultural leaders.

The Garifuna community—descended from Carib, Arawak, and West African people— lives along the beaches of Honduras and Nicaragua. They speak their own language and mainly fish for their livelihood. Eight years ago, a Garifuna man came to one of the Honduran universities. He became friends with a member of Humberto's church, and then became a believer. Humberto then began discipling this young man and training him for pastoral ministry. The man went back to his own people and raised up several more leaders from among them. The Garifuna community now has its own church.

Humberto has found that it's much easier to make friends among other people groups and then work through them to help them reach their own people. Bilingual and bicultural people are the ones who form the most effective bridges for bringing Jesus into new cultures.

Stay with it

As new apostolic leaders get started in ministry, they'll need training, resources, and coaching. What can do to support them and give their new ministries the best chance of success? Here's just a sampling of ideas:

- Provide orientation
- Train on-the-job
- Create space for reflection
- Ensure that every leader has a coach
- Identify leadership strengths and gaps
- Create personalized growth plans
- Track ministry progress
- Provide resources as needed
- Network apostolic leaders with one another for mutual support and learning
- Train apostolic leaders in coaching skills to help them develop new leaders in their ministries
- Provide new challenges
- Create an apprenticing system

One organization in Latin America takes an interesting approach to supporting and developing leaders. Ret al Camino, translated "Network on the Road," functions as a relational support system for missional leaders. Some leaders from the Dominican Republic started the network, and it now has representation in Honduras, Chile, Argentina, and Costa Rica. The group is based on strong relational connections between leaders who have a similar apostolic vision.

Depending on the locations involved, some leaders meet up once a month for dinner and coffee, and to spend time with one another building relationships. Although once in a while they have conferences or other formal gatherings, Ret al Camino is not programmatic—just organic and relational, a group of friends walking together on this journey of missional leadership.

Ret al Camino has moved beyond the common Latin American leadership style of a strong front man who has to keep an appearance of being in charge all the time. Instead, they support one another in close peer relationships, holding one another accountable, helping each other emotionally, and supporting one another in prayer. All of this is done in the context of apostolic vision, and has resulted in raising up new apostolic leaders across cultures.

> When I planted a church in Southern California, I was blessed to be part of a supportive peer coaching network. We met together once a month at In-N-Out Burger and shared our struggles and victories and prayed together. We learned from one another and supported each other. I drove almost 90 minutes each way to be with them. And it was absolutely worth it. Consider how you can network together apostolic leaders who can provide peer coaching and accountability to each other. The returns on this investment of time and effort will be exponential.
> - Dave

Keep growing

When we support our apostolic leaders so they can bridge cross-culturally into new people groups, we see spiritual transformation spread exponentially through different geographic regions and different segments of society. When that happens, we can see particular places where God seems to be moving. Those places—the fertile ground—are where we need to focus our energy and resources.

What steps can you take to capitalize on this momentum, in order to start more movements in other places? Consider how to keep your movement simple and reproducible so it continues to grow. Cut out the extras and the redundancies. Reflect on what's truly important and focus on duplicating that. In this way, you can streamline your organization. Simple, streamlined organizations multiply best.

A few years ago I had the privilege of traveling to India to train seventy church planting coordinators in coaching skills. By developing their leaders to coach more leaders, they focused on what was most important... and as a result, more than 1,300 churches were planted that year. How will you invest in the ongoing development, training, and coaching of movement leaders?

— Dave

You'll also need to let go. To see this work of God continue, you'll need to commission and release more apostolic leaders with your blessing to start new ministries and new movements. You can start doing this by forming collaborative relationships with other leaders, groups, and movements. And remember, you're not in control of the movement—God is. That's the nature of a movement. Rather than trying to control the multiplication process, release it and practice generosity.

Conclusion

From the vantage point of this last journey of multiplying movements, we can look back and see all four journeys as part of a coherent whole. We can view these journeys as one inside another inside another, ensuring that the DNA is in place all the way from the grassroots following of Jesus to multiplying movements that result in the praise around God's throne from all people groups and nations (see Rev. 7).

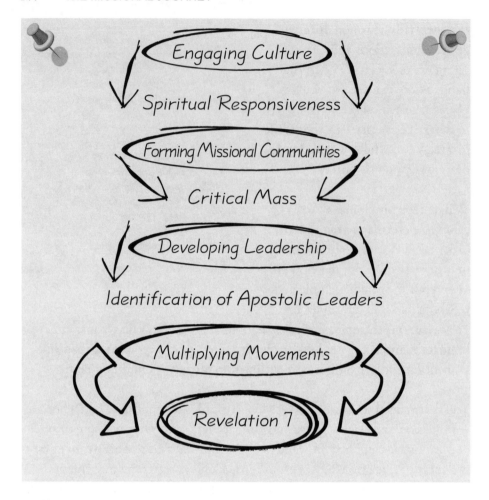

After this I looked, and there before me was a great multitude that no one could count, from every nation, tribe, people and language, standing before the throne and before the Lamb. They were wearing white robes and were holding palm branches in their hands. And they cried out in a loud voice: "Salvation belongs to our God, who sits on the throne, and to the Lamb" (Rev. 7:9–10).

The vision starts at the roots. The DNA works itself all the way through... from Jerusalem, to Judea and Samaria, to the ends of the earth. The ends of the earth are wherever we are—from downtown Los Angeles to the Australian outback to the Amazon River basin.

I recently met a man named Bud Simon who is part of a team with the Xingu Mission in the Amazon region of Brazil. In the face of the brokenness they're encountering—drunkenness, fights, domestic violence—God is working in power, and people are seeing the difference he makes as he brings healing, joy, love, and unity. There is a deep desire for life transformation.

Bud and his team engage in holistic ministry. They teamed with Brazilian leaders from the beginning, and are committed to raising up Brazilian leaders from new disciples. Through their Center for Regional Development they offer English classes, computer skills, literacy classes, a soccer school for kids, safety programs through the public schools, and medical help from doctors. Through these various ministries the center has touched 15,000 people—about twenty percent of the population. Their service has brought them the favor and goodwill of the people.

Just as it would be anywhere else, people aren't interested in what we say. They want to see what difference God really makes in the areas they care about. The service we do makes him real to them when they see the power of changed lives. The story Bud told me left me encouraged by the power of the God we serve. He describes a world akin to the one in Galatians:

> *The acts of the flesh are obvious: sexual immorality, impurity and debauchery; idolatry and witchcraft; hatred, discord, jealousy, fits of rage, selfish ambition, dissensions, factions and envy; drunkenness, orgies, and the like. I warn you, as I did before, that those who live like this will not inherit the kingdom of God.*

> *But the fruit of the Spirit is love, joy, peace, forbearance, kindness, goodness, faithfulness, gentleness and self-control. Against such things there is no law. Those who belong to Christ Jesus have crucified the flesh with its passions and desires. Since we live by the Spirit, let us keep in step with the Spirit. Let us not become conceited, provoking and envying each other (Gal. 5:19–26).*

Bud and his team see a radical transformation among those who come to faith in Jesus. Because the desire for relationship is high, it's assumed that new believers will come together for worship and encouragement. In the interior rural regions they sing songs of praise, listen to a chapter of the Bible on CD (due to low literacy rates), share, and pray together. It's a very simple, easily reproducible worship service.

In the urban center of Altamira, there are now about 1,200 people gathered in six churches. There are 37 home groups in the largest of these churches. The churches engage in ministry to those in the more remote rural areas where transportation is a problem, especially during the rainy season. They have teamed with a Brazilian leader with a strong apostolic gifting, and send out teams as itinerant ministers to do the works of Jesus: serving, equipping, and sharing the message of the gospel.

One time forty-five people packed into a 15-foot-by-15-foot room to hear about Jesus. Several people shared with no rush. When those listening were asked, "Do you want to receive Jesus?" one of the leaders responded, "We are not ready for that yet." That's when they realized this would be a collective decision of the community. Next time they asked, thirty people responded in faith and confessed their sins.

One man who had been living a life characterized by drinking and violence came to faith. His mentor in the faith is helping him stay on track with his spiritual growth, and helping him develop his opportunities to minister to others. His mentor has faith in his potential. Even from over a great distance they are able to connect once or twice a month to talk about what this new believer needs for the next steps in his development as a leader.

In this way, more Brazilian leaders are released and empowered. Over the last fifteen years, this group has started about twenty-five churches and thirty church plants in outlying areas. They define church plants as "smaller gatherings without formal leadership," but where disciple-making activities are happening. That's a total of fifty-five gatherings that include 2,500 people. One of the places where they serve is two hundred miles away, and transportation is difficult. The leaders in this rural area continue to get invitations to go further up the river where no church has been planted. They journey every three months into that region, and are excited to see what God is opening up there.

The more "urban" churches (in small cities and towns) are multiplying as well. One youth leader took over a dying church ten years ago. It's now at two hundred people, and has planted six other churches. This multiplication has even resulted in one or two great-granddaughter churches—that's four generations of multiplication so far. They have been sending out cross-cultural ministers to bridge across the very diverse people groups and subcultures who call Brazil home.

The Xingu Mission has been applying the principles of the missional journey to their culture and context. They work. We can apply them in our own diverse settings as well.

The journey of the Kingdom of God is not a straight line, but more a wandering road that must be discerned as we go. Much is impossible to predict beforehand, and many of the best things are things we stumble into—only to find that God has been preparing us for it all along.

> *Therefore, since we are surrounded by such a great cloud of witnesses, let us throw off everything that hinders and the sin that so easily entangles. And let us run with perseverance the race marked out for us, fixing our eyes on Jesus, the pioneer and perfecter of faith. For the joy set before him he endured the cross, scorning its shame, and sat down at the right hand of the throne of God. Consider him who endured such opposition from sinners, so that you will not grow weary and lose heart (Heb. 12:1-3).*

A vision for a different kind of church is going to require:
- *A different way of training*
- *A different kind of leader*
- *A different experience of community*
- *A different focus on disciple-making*
- *A different level of coaching*

What will you do to see this vision become reality?
        – Dave

The starting point for that race is right here. If we have a vision to see God do great things, if we have a vision for a church that is different—a church that brings authentic relationships, sacrificial service, and spiritual transformation to the world around it—we can start wherever we are. We may be starting with nothing, but that's okay. We may already be partway down a path, but now realizing there are pieces we've missed. That's okay, too—go back and fill them in.

This book provides a framework, but remember: God's going to surprise us as we travel along the way of this missional journey.

Journey Guide: Multiplying movements

Checklist: You are here

engaging culture

forming communities/churches

developing leadership

multiplying movements
- mobilizing apostolic leaders
- sending ministry teams
- crossing cultural barriers
- multiplying disciples, groups, and churches
- new movements starting new movements

Discussion questions: for you and your team

- What are you already doing?
- What's going well?
- What do you hear God saying to you?
- What reflections do you have on this chapter?

Guided prayer: for you and your team

Pray over the following passage of scripture. First, read it aloud slowly. Then pray over each line, allowing space and time between lines for meditation. Then read it slowly again for the third time.

"But you will receive power when the Holy Spirit comes on you; and you will be my witnesses in Jerusalem, and in all Judea and Samaria, and to the ends of the earth" (Acts 1:8).

End this time of prayer by inviting the Holy Spirit to come upon your team, and to reveal where he has laid your Jerusalem, Judea and Samaria, and the ends of the earth. Ask him how to begin reaching those areas.

Action planning guide

"Multiplying movements" coaching questions:

- How are you mobilizing apostolic leaders?
- How are you sending ministry teams?
- How are you crossing cultural barriers?
- How are you multiplying disciples, groups, and churches?
- How are you starting new movements?

Based on where you are in multiplying movements, work through the following questions and action steps together with your team:

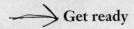 **Get ready**

Action points:

- Discern where God is working
- Identify proven multipliers—those who are making disciples who make disciples
- Network with others who are engaging culture, forming missional communities, and developing leaders
- Pray for harvest workers—expand your prayer base
- Ask God to enlarge your vision

Questions to discuss with your team:

- How can you move beyond "accidental" church planting to intentionally starting new disciple-making communities?
- Where is your starting point?

 **Get going**

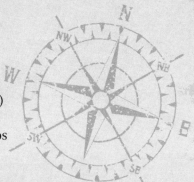

Action points:

- Raise up all types of leaders (APEST)
- Multiply compassion ministries
- Look beyond your own people groups

Questions to discuss with your team:

- What units do we need to multiply?
- Where do we sense God calling us to start?

→ Stay with it

Action points:

- Be generous with training, resources, and coaches
- Network apostolic leaders with one another for mutual support and learning
- Cut the extras and redundancies
- Shift leadership styles when necessary

Questions to discuss with your team:

- How will you track progress?
- How will you measure success?

→ Keep growing

Action points:

- Intentionally cross bridges and barriers: language, cultural, social, economic, racial, etc.
- Spot apostolic leaders, especially those willing to cross cultural lines
- Invest in bicultural and bilingual leaders
- Always think "simple and reproducible"
- Release apostolic leaders

Questions to discuss with your team:

- How can you best practice generosity?
- How can you help others multiply?

Chapter 9

The role of network leaders: what you can do from the top down

This book has been written to create a broad-strokes vision of what a grassroots movement looks like from the ground up. That's an ideal approach if you're starting a new ministry or planting a new church. But let's say you're a network leader. Maybe you oversee a group of churches, a region, or a denomination. Instead of looking at things from the ground up, you're looking at things from the top down. You still need the vision painted in the rest of this book, but you also need to figure out how you can best expend your energy to make this vision come alive. What can you do from the top?

If you're a network leader, you've already realized that your role is to empower networks of multiplying churches. You probably already have a number of tools that help you spot the right people, develop them, resource them, etc.—and those are helpful tools. Yet, if you're already overseeing a network of churches, the reality is: Every church probably isn't on the same page you are. Many of them simply aren't ready or willing to go where you want to lead them. You're responsible to care for all of them, yet you also have this desire to help your churches engage in missional ministry. How can you move forward?

As network leaders, you have a significant role to play as you lead your organization on the missional journey. In this section, we're going to highlight the key result areas a missional network leader needs to focus on, in order to lead your network of churches on the missional journey.

Key result areas:

- Identifying which congregations to work with
- Developing and resourcing leaders
- Selecting and training coaches
- Creating a supportive process for pilot projects
- Leading change

Identifying which congregations to work with

The very idea of deciding which congregations (or ministries, communities, or churches) to work with may sound strange. Shouldn't you be leading all of them along the missional journey? That would be wonderful, but in most cases it's not realistic—especially at the beginning of the journey. In the parable of the sower, Jesus recognized that not everyone would be ready to hear his gospel message. The same is true today.

While a large crowd was gathering and people were coming to Jesus from town after town, he told this parable: "A farmer went out to sow his seed. As he was scattering the seed, some fell along the path; it was trampled on, and the birds ate it up. Some fell on rocky ground, and when it came up, the plants withered because they had no moisture. Other seed fell among thorns, which grew up with it and choked the plants. Still other seed fell on good soil. It came up and yielded a crop, a hundred times more than was sown" (Luke 8:4–8).

At some point, leaders can begin to think that they know what they're doing and don't need any help, thank you. Focus on working with churches that actually are willing and ready to learn. No matter how hard you try to help, some churches won't want your help.

— Dave

While we also can invite all of our churches to join us, the likely reality is that not all of them will want to join us. So how do we handle these differing responses? How do we sort out who's ready and who's not? I call it "sorting the soils." We assess our churches—determining their readiness and receptivity, and sorting them by category. In his explanation of the parable of the sower, Jesus determined the various levels of receptivity, the blockages, and what was needed.

> *"This is the meaning of the parable: The seed is the word of God. Those along the path are the ones who hear, and then the devil comes and takes away the word from their hearts, so that they may not believe and be saved. Those on the rocky ground are the ones who receive the word with joy when they hear it, but they have no root. They believe for a while, but in the time of testing they fall away. The seed that fell among thorns stands for those who hear, but as they go on their way they are choked by life's worries, riches and pleasures, and they do not mature. But the seed on good soil stands for those with a noble and good heart, who hear the word, retain it, and by persevering produce a crop" (Luke 8:11-15).*

There are different levels of receptivity, based on soils alone. Sometimes the soil is good, and the church is immediately receptive to missional initiatives—all they need is a challenge or some information and resourcing. Sometimes the soil is hard—like hearts are hard—and they won't respond at all. Other churches get excited about the idea of being missional, but their roots are shallow, and they wipe out at the first sign of adversity. In many cases, churches get distracted from moving in a missional direction by other things that vie for their attention: crisis, leadership problems, programs, buildings, etc.

I've found that this last scenario is especially true in larger churches. Large churches often have the most difficulty moving in a missional direction because something else always absorbs their attention—new staff coming or going, crisis happening somewhere, deaths, buildings, programs. It's hard to keep the attention focused on the journey toward becoming more missional. There are certainly exceptions, but I've found that

It's amazing how easily a building program can take a church off mission. Even when the justification of purchasing property and constructing a building is to advance a church's mission, oftentimes the pursuit of the building becomes the mission.

Buildings are tools to accomplish mission. The mission is making disciples. Consider that buildings can become an obstacle to missional activity. I call this edificialism - A preoccupation with property and buildings as a measure of legitimacy.
- Dave

smaller or mid-sized churches tend to be more fruitful on the whole.

Here's an exercise to help you sort the soils. In some cases, you may need to do some guesswork or have conversations with the senior leaders of specific congregations. It can be helpful to have a working chart as you go; you can always adjust a congregation's status as it changes.

Sort the churches you oversee into the following six categories:

- Hostile: actively blocking movement toward becoming more missional
- Resistant: don't make me (digging in heels)
- Passive: ignoring all attempts to interest them in the missional journey
- Cultivatable: could eventually move in a more missional direction if you work with them for two or three years, but not in this next wave
- Receptive: conceptually embrace the missional journey, but may need help to figure out timing, ownership, and how to go about it. Not ready yet, but could be in a year or so.
- Ready: wants to commit, buy in; if resourced well, is ready to embark on the missional journey

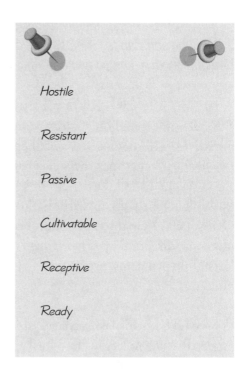

Once you've completed your chart, take note of the following things:

- the sizes and the ages of the churches
- the relative level of health of each church
- your relationship with the senior leaders of each church

- where you spend most of your time
- which churches you're unsure where to place on the chart

This can be an eye-opening experience. In some cases, conversations with pastors may be in order to better determine where each church is and what it needs. The key person to process is the pastor. He or she is often the gatekeeper for whether the missional journey moves forward or is blocked. There is often a fear of loss of control that can manifest itself through either active or passive resistance.

Taking time to reflect on where each of your churches are at can help you better prioritize as you lead your network. It can also help you tailor your approach to each church, depending on its needs.

Developing and resourcing leaders

Another area that's critical for network leaders to focus on is leadership development. There is no church or group of churches I've ever spoken with that has said they don't need more leadership development. The key question, then, is what kind of leadership development they need.

If your goal is to move your network of churches in a missional direction, you probably don't need more seminars or conferences. You have those already. You probably need a more relational approach in keeping with the nature of missional ministry. You need coaching. Coaching is the central thread of leadership development—the piece that holds all the rest together. Without coaching, all the rest of our efforts will continue to unravel: the classes, the books, the meetings. No matter how well we do them, they don't work without the relational connection that coaching provides.

As a church planter who was blessed to have a coach from the very beginning. I celebrate how true this is. Every church planter. and every missional leader. needs a coach. Yet it's amazing how many don't have one. And the result is often loneliness and despair.

If you don't have a coach. get one. If you do have a coach, thank your coach for walking with you in the journey.
- Dave

What happens when we try to do leadership development without coaching? Let's take a look at some of the most common scenarios.

- *Recruiting instead of developing:* The most extreme response is giving up trying to develop leaders at all. Instead, we look for ready-made leaders who are fully trained, self-motivating, self-correcting, self-sustaining, and need no investment. Not only is there an extreme shortage of such people, but we contribute nothing to the Kingdom with this approach. Our energy is focused internally, trying to get enough leaders to meet our own organization's needs.

- *Training classroom-style only:* In many ministries, developing leaders is done exclusively in a classroom context. Without experience, practice, and a feedback loop incorporated through coaching, leaders often have great difficulty translating what they've learned in the class to real-life ministry situations.

- *Training and releasing:* Another common problem we face when coaching is left out of the picture is the "train and release" phenomenon. After we have trained leaders (usually in groups and in a classroom), we consider the job done. We send them out and never check up on them unless something goes wrong.

- *Processing leaders in groups:* Some who do understand that follow-up after training is necessary try to do it in groups, rather than one-on-one. It seems more efficient to hold leader meetings and process them in groups. However, this approach lacks the focus, quality, and direct relevance that one-on-one coaching provides.

- *Not challenging and releasing leaders to what God has next for them:* If we're focused on perpetuating our organization and don't have a strong coaching system in place, it's easy to miss what God may be calling people toward next. Sometimes the next stage of development requires that person to move on. We can't hang onto people—they need to be free to leave our ministry and go wherever God maybe calling them.

And then there's leadership development that does work: People learn best when they...

- have someone to come alongside them
- engage experientially through on-the-job training
- can focus on both life and ministry skills
- take time to reflect on their experiences
- receive a consistent investment of time and energy over the long haul

Effective network leaders need to invest at least twenty percent of their time in coaching leaders. If that's not the case for us, it likely means we're either spending too much time pushing papers or too much time doing all the work of the ministry ourselves. We'll also need to invest some time in training new coaches. If coaching is truly the central thread of leadership development—the one piece without which nothing else holds together—you'll need a lot of coaches. You can't do it alone. You'll need to be intentional about raising and multiplying quality coaches within your ministry.

Selecting and training coaches

If coaching is the core discipline for the effective resourcing of the missional journey, how do you raise and multiply quality coaches within your network? Whatever type of training and developing system you use to raise up coaches, be sure to incorporate the following elements:

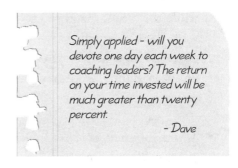

Simply applied - will you devote one day each week to coaching leaders? The return on your time invested will be much greater than twenty percent.

- Dave

- *Select the right people:* Before multiplying anything, you'll want to know that what you're multiplying is of high quality. Carefully select those people you want trained as coaches. Start with your best people.

- *Know what qualities you're trying to produce:* If we want to reproduce high quality coaches, we need to know first what qualities, competencies or skills we're trying to create in them. Once we have this list, we can tailor our training process accordingly.

- *Make the learning experiential:* To make sure the coaches we train are fully equipped, the training process itself must be experiential and hands-on. Most coach training is not coach training at all—it is downloading of content. What works best is to have coaches-in-training come to the seminar having already mastered the content by having read the material beforehand and having talked it through with their coach-mentor. The training time can then be used to interact and practice coaching skills.

- *Coach people as they practice coaching:* Good training also offers hands-on coach-mentoring. The principle behind this is that you learn coaching best when you've experienced it. After the training event, the coach-in-training coaches two people while the coach-mentor helps walk them through that process. Together, they reflect on the coaching process while doing it.

> I started coaching because I received the benefit of coaching. I realized what a difference it made as I planted a church—and I wanted to pay it forward by coaching other church planters.
>
> I also discovered that developing my skills as a coach increased my impact. Not everyone who receives coaching should become a coach. Select a few who express a desire to coach others, and invest in their ongoing training and development.
>
> - Dave

- *Measure outcomes to ensure quality:* After training we'll also need to circle back to measure competencies—to see if what we're doing in our training process is achieving the desired outcomes. An outcome-based assessment process needs to be put in place to assure that the training process is working as designed.

- *Use a reproducible process:* Fortunately, more potential coaches are found among those receiving coaching. In this way, the system is sustainable. When the pool of future leadership comes out of those who've been helped, that's how a movement starts developing.

Imagine the potential of having coaches available at every level of your denomination, so that everyone is getting the help, connection, and resourcing they need—the new church planters, the denominational leaders, the local church pastors... even small-group leaders and new converts. Consider some of the potential applications:

- Discipleship of new believers
- Personal and ministry development for emerging leaders
- Pastoral and leader development
- Follow-up after seminars or training events
- Cultivation of church health
- Start-ups and multiplication of new missional ministries

Imagine the potential for missional growth. After all, we don't want coaches for the sake of having coaches—we want coaches for the sake of mission. Coaches support mission.

Creating a supportive process for pilot projects

One of the most important things you can do as a network leader is provide a supportive environment for pilot projects. Sponsor and support new compassion ministries—new ways of serving and living missionally together. Pilot projects, by their very nature, are somewhat experimental. Sometimes they work and sometimes they don't. Therefore, permission to experiment— and possibly to fail—is essential for innovation. Consider the needs in the various communities your network serves. How can your churches be empowered to make a difference in those areas? How can you support them?

Remember, with pilot projects, that not everyone has to get on board. If you have one church that wants to do something missional in its community, provide the coaching and support necessary to help them do it. And when there is success, broadcast it to the other churches in the network. Successes create powerful vision-casting tools, and lay the groundwork for replicating what worked to more churches.

Leading change

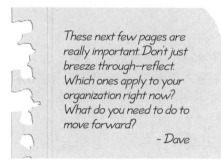

These next few pages are really important. Don't just breeze through—reflect. Which ones apply to your organization right now? What do you need to do to move forward?

– Dave

Leading a network of churches along the missional journey will require all the leadership skills you have—particularly skills for leading change. Whenever there is any kind of change to be navigated, this specific set of leadership skills comes into play. If you're a network leader, most of these skills will already look quite familiar to you. However, consider specifically how you can apply them to guiding your network of churches in missional directions.

Regardless of the type of change we're trying to implement, the same common barriers to change remain in our way. We'll organize our thinking here through a problem-solution approach. Below are some of the most common barriers that hold back change, followed by the leadership dynamics required to address that barrier effectively. As you read this section, think of your own ministry situation. What's standing in the way of your progress toward missional transformation? Put a checkmark beside the dynamics you see at work in your situation.

Barriers to Change

Problem: Corporate ADD

Sometimes organizations are afflicted by corporate ADD—attention deficit disorder. We engage in a pattern of starting something, losing focus, starting something different, and so on. When we behave this way repeatedly, we're essentially training our people not to take us seriously. They know that if they simply wait and do nothing, this whole missional thing will probably blow over and something new will come down the road. There's no need to pay attention, there's no need to take action—if they just wait a while, the problem will go away. Essentially, we've trained our people not to listen to us.

Solution: Tenacious focus

So what's the remedy? Forget about quick fixes. We need a tenacious focus—a long-term commitment to missional transformation in our network so our people will begin to understand that we're sticking with it. Good things don't come easily. The kind of deep change we're talking about here—missional transformation—will require a deep, long-term commitment of time and energy. With real focus, the seeds of transformation in an existing organization can be established in a three-year period, but then those seeds must be cultivated in years four through seven, so that in years eight through ten the change can be truly established as a part of the organizational culture.

Problem: Convoy mentality

As denominations or networks, we tend to believe that for organizational change to take place, we must first get everyone on the same page, ready to move along in the same direction. We will all go together. Until everyone is ready to move, no one moves. While it would be nice to have everyone move forward together, it's simply not realistic. Not everyone is ready or willing to move forward. If we try to force the issue, we often run into significant resistance or end up watering down what we want to accomplish for the sake of consensus.

Solution: Build an opt-in guiding coalition

We can create additional environments within our organization that aren't pre-committed, but opt-in. Participation is voluntary and membership consists of those who are passionately committed to investing in missional transformation. Gideon didn't need a large army for victory in battle, just a few who believed in the mission and were willing. The others were not kicked out of the army—just sent home. They weren't needed. Organizational change doesn't happen without a guiding coalition moving that change forward. We don't need everyone—just those who are open and willing to try new things. Start small and build from there. Momentum will build as you go.

Problem: Education beyond obedience

A common breakdown occurs when we try to cram everything someone could possibly someday need to know into their orientation or training. We overload them with information, and their practice doesn't have a chance to catch up. Essentially, we educate people beyond their obedience. We teach them to pre-think everything before they act at all.

Solution: Experiential learning

Instead of thinking our way into a new way of acting, we need to act ourselves into a new way of thinking. People learn best—especially about missional living and missional ministry—through the crucible of experience. Even the knowledge pieces—which can be taught in a classroom—are best learned when they're based on a real need that people are currently experiencing. We can give them just enough to get started— bite-sized pieces that align with their current situation. That approach allows individual churches and leaders to learn experientially as they go, providing the needed content a little at a time.

Problem: Event focus

One major mistake we make is thinking that a good event, all by itself, will bring about change. We believe that we can gather people in groups, inspire them and train them, and our goals will be accomplished. Providing a good orientation is helpful, but it only takes us partway. If seminars could do it, we'd be done by now.

Solution: Process focus

We don't need another event. What we need is the follow-up that takes our people the rest of the way through the process. What we need is follow-up at each stage along the way, step by step. Some form of relational coaching—monthly or more frequent—needs to be offered as a piece of that follow-up. Often people aren't sure what the next step is after an event; they need someone along the way to help them figure it out and help them stay on track. Life itself has a tendency to distract us from what's truly important. Lasting transformation is not just about inspiring people, but about providing the support that empowers them to experience true change over time. In that sense, what happens for follow-up is actually more important than what happens at the event itself.

Problem: Working in isolation

Working, living, and ministering in isolation is one of the most crippling challenges ministry leaders face. Many would-be missional leaders get road-blocked on their way to reaching their goals, simply due to lack of connection with others. It sounds simple, but it's essential—we need other people along the way with us. We need additional perspectives and fresh ideas. We need sounding boards and a place to process our thoughts. We need to feel like we're connected to something bigger. All of this is essential to moving forward. Without intentionally creating an environment that allows connection with others around these kinds of ideas—something with set aside time—many good intentions come to nothing. We often have very limited opportunity to reflect on our experience and learn from others.

Solution: Gather like-minded people together

One of the best ways to overcome isolation is by intentionally gathering people together on similar journeys. These can be small gatherings of denominational leaders (even when they're from different denominations), groups of senior pastors, gatherings of missional church planters, or grassroots level leaders coming together for support and encouragement. These gatherings are a huge gift to our leaders. By creating these opportunities for processing with peers, we're allowing people to start thinking outside the box and begin innovating. We also become a blessing to our entrepreneurial leaders—whose success is critical to our own success.

Problem: Too high too fast

Often we set the bar too high too fast. An athlete training for the high jump wouldn't start with the bar seven feet high; he or she would start much lower and then work his or her way up with intentional challenges that require an appropriate amount of stretch. Whenever a certain height was no longer challenging, the bar would be raised. Similarly, someone who can't throw a party for his neighbors can't be expected to be commissioned as a community missionary. Someone who has never dished out soup to the poor should certainly not set her eyes on starting a whole ministry to them. Setting the bar too high too quickly results in people failing and feeling discouraged, overwhelmed, and frustrated.

Solution: Incremental goals

We need to set small, manageable goals in ministry. By building up to the goal with smaller steps and celebrating along the way, we create an atmosphere of encouragement and momentum. Everyone understands how to celebrate accomplishing a big goal. What we often don't understand is that we're more likely to meet our goal in the first place if we celebrate along the way. Celebrating the small victories creates a significant motivation for people to keep trying.

Problem: Contentment with the status quo

The lack of a sense of urgency is one of the primary reasons missional transformation doesn't happen. If we're satisfied with the status quo, there is no motivation for change.

Solution: Cultivate a clear and compelling vision

Instead, we need passionate commitment to a big vision—a vision that is clear and compelling. Look ahead fifteen to twenty years. If God had his way, what would look different? Picture the new things that would be emerging—new ministries and initiatives, not just revitalization. Once you have this clear and compelling vision in mind, paint that picture for the churches in your network. You'll need to help them uncover their dissatisfaction with the status quo, and to talk about the vision in such a way that it takes hold of people. Help them want to make the sacrifice and take the risks, by moving them toward this new vision of a preferred future.

Problem: Lack of example from the leadership

If leaders don't model missional living and ministry, it isn't really a value. Just as those in a congregation look to the pastor to see what's truly important, the pastors of the churches in your network are looking to you to see what's really important. And they're not looking at what you say, but at what you do and at how you invest your time. What will they see?

Solution: Model the change you want to see

In missional ministry, the essential starting point is to lead by example. Without that foundational piece in place, any broader organizational change won't go anywhere. So, what are you doing personally? Just because you're a denominational executive doesn't mean you can't be a volunteer in a food pantry. Serve. Get involved in missional initiatives. Build relationships with those who don't already know Jesus. Tell personal stories about what you're involved in. When people hear what you're doing, it will encourage them to get involved, too.

Can you envision the missional journey? Missional leaders are raised up from new converts and begin multiplying themselves. Systems of leadership development begin growing at the very grassroots of the movement. People are being helped toward growth in discipleship and maturity. Compassion ministries are formed. Surrounding communities begin experiencing transformation and a new understanding of what Jesus is all about. Soon, congregations begin branching out to form more congregations. The whole region of churches is revitalized and growing. You can see the Kingdom of God expanding here on earth.

Do you want to be a part of implementing that? Do you want to find ways to organize and focus your network of churches in a more missional direction? This chapter provides some good, practical starting points. You could also give this book to leaders of your churches, to help them cast vision for the missional journey.

The bulk of practical church-planting resources, however, will be coming out in our upcoming resource, The *Missional Church Planter's Toolkit*. Check out ***www.missionaltoolkit.com*** to stay abreast of the most current resources.

> Keep in mind that coaches will make a difference in working with the new churches being started, but they also are needed to walk alongside parent churches that are giving birth to new churches. Coaching is vital for both the birthing and recovery processes. Coaches can help to ensure the healthy birth weight of a new church—as well as the continued health of the parent congregation, as they prepare to give birth again.
> - Dave

The very most important thing you can do, right now, is to get coaching. Get connected. Every journey is different, and you need other people walking alongside you if you hope to see your vision become a reality.

Blessings on the journey ahead of you.

Journey Guide: Network leaders

Missional network leaders empower networks of multiplying churches to engage in missional ministry through engaging the culture, forming missional communities, developing leadership, and multiplying movements.

Prayer Guide

Questions for prayer and reflection:

- As you read this chapter, what struck a chord?
- What opportunities do you see?
- Where might God want you to start?

⟶ Get ready

- Listen to the Holy Spirit as you assess the churches in your network
- Prayerfully identify each congregation's readiness and receptivity
- "Sort the soils" based on the following categories:
  o Hostile
  o Resistant
  o Passive
  o Cultivatable
  o Receptive
  o Ready
- Reflect on the following aspects:
  o Sizes and ages of the churches
  o Relative level of health of each church
  o Your relationship with the senior leaders of each church
  o Where you spend most of your time
  o Which churches you're unsure of where to place
- Prioritize which churches you'll approach first
- Tailor your approach depending on needs

⟶ Get going

- Resist all temptation to abandon coaching as you develop leaders
- Avoid the following pitfalls:

  o Recruiting instead of developing
  o Training classroom-style only
  o Training and releasing

o Processing leaders in groups, rather than one-on-one
o Not challenging and releasing leaders to what God has next for them

- Develop more and better coaches

  o Start with your best people
  o Know what qualities/skills you're reproducing
  o Make all learning experiential
  o Coach new coaches as they practice coaching
  o Use an outcome-based assessment process
  o Reproduce coaches out of the pool of those being coached

⟶ Stay with it

- Keep supporting leaders through coaching—at every level of your network
- Give permission (if necessary) to experiment
- Initiate pilot projects with those willing to take risks
- Provide coaching for leaders of pilot projects
- Broadcast stories of effective missional ministry throughout your network
- Lay relational groundwork for replicating what's working

⟶ Keep growing

- Ensure that you're receiving the coaching you need to keep growing as a network leader
- Pray like crazy
- Reflect on these common barriers and develop a plan to overcome them
  o Corporate ADD
  o Convoy mentality
  o Education beyond obedience
  o Event focus
  o Working in isolation
  o Too high too fast
  o Contentment with the status quo
  o Lack of example from the leadership
- Anticipate the Kingdom of God expanding
- Celebrate all that God is doing

Appendix A

Websites:

The following websites and books may be helpful to you on your missional journey. The listing below can get you started, but there's a lot of other great stuff out there. You can find more at *www.missionaltoolkit.com*.

- **www.missionaltoolkit.com**: This website, newly launched with this book, will be the home of many forthcoming resources for those on the missional journey, including the soon-to-be-released *Missional Church Planters Toolkit*.

- **www.mycoachlog.com**: a simple process for facilitating your coaching relationships with individuals and/or teams. MyCoachLog makes your coaching more effective with less work, while keeping all of your information in one place.

- **www.loganleadership.com**: your central hub for leadership development. This site includes information on coaching, consulting, and upcoming training events and is home to an online resource store and Bob's blog.

- **www.missionalchallenge.com**: Dave DeVries' website includes information on training events and additional resources, as well as insights from his blog.

- **www.missio.us**: Hugh Halter and Matt Smay, providing thought leadership and resources for the missional movement.

- **www.journeytogethernow.com**: designed to resource anyone who wants to live incarnationally and missionally as they follow in the footsteps of Jesus. This site includes a map of the 9 footsteps of Jesus with information, coaching questions, and downloadable guides.

Books:

- *Tangible Kingdom Primer* by Hugh Halter and Matt Smay
- *Barefoot Church Primer* by Brandon Hatmaker
- *Six-word Lessons to Discover Missional Living* by Dave DeVries
- *Making Life Count: Following Jesus in the 21st Century*, by Robert E. Logan and Tara Miller
- *From Followers to Leaders* by Robert E. Logan and Tara Miller
- *Coaching 101: Discover the Power of Coaching* by Robert E. Logan and Sherilyn Carlton

All items in the following appendices are downloadable at: *www.loganleadership.com/resources*

Appendix B

ViaCordis Life Transformation Group (LTG)

ViaCordis is a growing network of multi-cultural leaders and associated churches who journey together to start and multiply communities of Jesus followers. Within ViaCordis we have formed smaller Life Transformation Groups (LTGs) that meet weekly for personal accountability in our spiritual growth. Each LTG reads passages of scripture prior to our weekly gathering. When we gather, we focus on growing in holiness and spiritual maturity, and we pray for one another and for those who are not followers of Jesus. Once our group of two or three people reaches four people, we covenant to multiply and form two groups so that others may come to know Christ and become established in the faith.

Structure of LTG meeting:

- Ask one another the questions on the bottom of this sheet.
- Pray for one another and for unbelievers:
    o I pray Lord that you draw ___ to yourself. (John 6:44)
    o I pray Lord that you give me the opportunity, the courage and the right words to share the truth with____ (Col. 4:3–6).
- Decide what biblical book you all will read between now and next week:
    o Recommendation: Read a total of 25–30 chapters weekly.
    o Note: If it is a shorter book, read it a number of times. If it is a longer book, divide the reading into several parts.

LTG Conversation Questions

Describe your interaction with God this week.
- Joys, struggles, breakthroughs with God

How did you share Jesus with others?
- By your actions
- By your words

What temptations did you face this week? How did you respond?
- Sinful thoughts or behaviors
- Examples: lust, greed, envy, dishonesty, gluttony, laziness, wrath, pride, etc.

What did the Holy Spirit teach you through your scripture reading this week?
- Insights
- Guidance

What next steps does God want you to take personally? With others?

Appendix C

The ViaCordis 12 Life Commitments

Below are the life commitments made by the members of ViaCordis. Subsequent pages include the behavioral expressions of these commitments, as well as coaching questions they ask one another to help each other stay on track. You're welcome to use this material, as you continue on your own journey of incarnational living.

Love God

Relationship: deepening our experience of God
Transformation: becoming more like Jesus
Responsiveness: following the guidance of Holy Spirit

Love others

Authenticity: being genuine and honest in all areas of our lives
Respect: valuing people wherever they are
Involvement: engaging relationally with those around us
Service: being the hands and feet of Jesus

Make disciples

Discern: discovering in whom God is working
Explore: purposeful conversations about the gospel
Invite: encouraging people to become followers of Jesus
Establish: baptize and teach loving obedience to Jesus
Multiply: help new followers make more followers

Expressions of the 12 Life Commitments

The following expressions are the outcomes that ViaCordis is trying to produce in its leaders. An initial coaching question is included for each of the 12 Life Commitments. Through consistent, focused coaching conversations, leaders can reflect upon where they are and how God wants them to grow personally and develop their ministry.

Love God

Relationship: How are you deepening your experience with God?
- interacting with scripture
- deepening honest dialogue with God
- increasing our awareness of God's presence
- experiencing awe and worship of God
- seeking to know and understand God
- bringing our whole selves to God

Transformation: How is God changing your life?
- reflecting on ourselves and our experiences
- growing in our understanding of what Jesus is like
- repenting and confessing our sin
- renewing our mind and heart
- growing in holiness
- living out new priorities and changed behavior

Responsiveness: How has the Holy Spirit been prompting you?
- practicing whole-life worship
- demonstrating the fruit of the Spirit
- cultivating a heart of compassion
- discerning God's voice and where he's working
- seeking and following God's calling for our life
- checking what we hear against scripture and our community
- acting in faith through loving obedience

Love others

Authenticity: In what ways are you being genuine with those around you?
- demonstrating consistency between private and public life
- being full of grace and truth
- living by Kingdom values rather than by conventional expectations
- displaying appropriate transparency about our struggles and our joys
- deepening our understanding of who God has made us to be
- being willing to ask for forgiveness or help when needed

Respect: How have you had opportunity to value people?
- seeing and calling out the image of God in others
- valuing the contributions of others
- practicing active listening in the context of open dialogue
- seeking to understand others who are different from ourselves
- accepting people regardless of their condition, position, circumstances or choices
- treating others as we want to be treated

Involvement: How are you relationally engaged with others?
- taking initiative in developing relationships
- prioritizing an appropriate level of investment in others
- creating ways to practice the "one-anothers" of scripture
- celebrating well in all of our relationships
- entering the environments of others and inviting them into ours
- praying with and for others
- honoring our commitments

Service: How have you been the hands and feet of Jesus?
- actively ministering to the oppressed and the needy
- standing in the way of injustice
- serving humbly and joyfully in creative ways
- giving of our time and our resources
- using our gifts to serve others creatively
- teaming with others to change our communities
- following the promptings of the Spirit to do what Jesus would do

Make disciples

Discern: In whom do you see God working?
- praying that God would show us where he is at work
- seeking to understand the cultural distinctives of others
- recognizing opportunities for spiritual conversation
- respond to promptings of the Spirit to connect with others

Explore: What conversations have you had about spiritual things?
- deepening our relationships with pre-Christians and their networks
- asking questions about the spiritual journeys of others and listening
- sharing our own spiritual journey with Jesus
- inviting them to consider the claims of Christ

Invite: Who have you encouraged to become followers of Jesus?
- explaining the good news and the way of Jesus
- interacting with peoples' questions and concerns
- encouraging people to follow Jesus
- guiding people to repent, believe, and acknowledge Jesus as Lord

Establish: How are you helping new believers follow Jesus?
- baptizing new believers as quickly and publicly as possible
- involving new believers in the life of the church
- establishing an ongoing discipleship process
- asking new believers to share their journey with Jesus with their family and friends

Multiply: How are you helping new followers make more followers?
- praying for increased receptivity with their networks of people
- identifying pre-Christian people of peace that can influence others
- engaging in coaching and being coached
- continuing to reach others and form new communities of Jesus followers
- praying for more generations of disciples and leaders

Appendix D

The Path

For more information on the metaphor of the path, see the book *From Followers to Leaders*, by Robert E. Logan and Tara Miller. A brief outline, with some basic coaching questions, is given below.

Motivation: the parking lot

The parking lot is where people are waiting around, sitting and deciding whether they even want to take the journey. Our role as missional leaders, at this stage, is to help them reflect on the vision and count the cost. Parking-lot questions include:

- What's the destination?
- What are the risks and rewards?
- What training and support is available?
- Is it worth the effort? Do we want to go?
- Are we willing to commit?

Orientation: the trailhead

At the trailhead, we provide a general overview of what will be involved so people understand what they're signing up for. We orient them and help them know what to expect. Trailhead questions include:

- So where exactly are we going again?
- Who else is going on this journey?
- What do we want to accomplish?
- What's going to happen once we get started?
- What support is available along the way?

Show-how training: the beginning of the trail

At the beginning of the trail we need to help people learn what to do. We can model and teach some basic skills using "show-how training," the approach we see Jesus using in the scriptures. In this way, we can develop others by gradually increasing their involvement in various aspects of ministry. We'll expand on this concept throughout the rest of the book. Beginning of the trail questions include:

- Which way do we go?
- How do we get started?
- What obstacles need to be overcome?
- What's the first goal/milestone?

Ongoing coaching: along the path

Coaching forms the central thread of the entire path. Coaching means coming alongside someone in a relational way to help them discover God's agenda for their life and ministry and bring that vision to fruition. This process takes place directly during the show-how training. It occurs in a more individualized fashion along the way as progress is made, and in a peer-coaching context within the networks. Coaching celebrates progress and everything moving forward. Along-the-path questions include:

- What progress can we celebrate?
- What's the next intermediate goal?
- What mid-course corrections do we need to make?
- How can we improve?

Networks: campfire conversations

A network is a supportive, relational environment that facilitates personal growth and mission. Good networks mean that we're not walking the path of ministry alone—we are helping each other along the way. They provide support for those who are committed to traveling down the same path together. Campfire questions include:

- What are others doing?
- How can we learn from them?
- What can we offer them?
- How can we support each other?

Destination: end-of-the-trail celebration

Accomplishment calls for celebration. Reaching our destination is a time for celebrating all the hard work, and for recognizing how far we've come. It's a time for reflection on the path we've taken and the paths that still lie ahead. Destination questions include:

- What have we accomplished?
- What have we learned?
- What is the next opportunity?
- Who else can join us?

Appendix E

What makes a good missional coach?

How do we know whether someone is a good coach for missional leaders? In addition to strong general coaching skills, here are the competencies to look for and/or instill:

1. Principle-based perspective: Thorough understanding of the basic principles that undergird incarnational missional ministry

   - Possesses a working knowledge of missional literature
   - Stays current with practices and available resources
   - Can identify, articulate, and apply the core principles of missional living
   - Understands how to integrate these principles with everyday life
   - Utilizes multiple methods and approaches to foster missional ministry

2. Credibility and connection: The ability to connect helpfully and relationally with missional leaders
   - Personally engages in a missional lifestyle
   - Draws from an experience of active involvement in missional ministry
   - Creates freedom for the leader's unique vision, motivation and calling
   - Facilitates the leader feeling understood, supported and not manipulated
   - Walks with the missional leader through relational and financial decisions

3. Creative contextualization: A capacity for outside-the-box thinking about what kind of approaches will work in a particular context
   - Able to help leaders translate their vision into a workable plan of action
   - Understands intercultural dynamics and how to bridge them
   - Focuses on underlying principles rather than forms
   - Asks questions that help the leader articulate appropriate contextualization
   - Helps the leader visualize clear paths for building missional community

4. Sustainable organization: The ability to help leaders develop and adapt sustainable systems as their missional ministry grows
   - Helps design structures that will help rather than hinder missional ministry
   - Strategically makes use of organizational change dynamics to translate obstacles into opportunities
   - Walks through financial and budgeting decisions with missional leaders
   - Helps missional leaders navigate the larger systems in which they work (denominational, legal, supervisory)
   - Utilizes clear a clear tracking system for all coaching relationships

5. Multiplication outlook: Focuses on the reproducible nature of missional living
   - Surfaces the issue of multiplication regularly, as a result of it being a deeply held value
   - Facilitates reflection on how to make disciples, in a way that contributes to a larger movement
   - Equips leader to multiply missional communities and leaders
   - Reframes success as the fruit of ministry being the future of ministry
   - Expands the vision for one's own ministry being only one piece of the larger Kingdom

Acknowledgements

How to even begin to acknowledge all the people who have journeyed together with me over the years? I think of mentors from years ago such as Carl George and John Wimber. I think of teams I've served with—my partnership with Rob Acker and Byron Spradlin at Community Baptist Church and with Steve Ogne at Church Resource Ministries. I think of my spiritual family at ViaCordis, especially Jon and Taylor Van-Bruggen who helped us to get off to a great start. This faith community has had a profound effect on my thinking as we've journeyed together with an incarnational missional focus for several years now.

In some ways it feels like God has been preparing me my whole life for this book. So many people have had a hand in shaping my life it would be impossible to list all of those influences. So here are specifically some people I'd like to thank in direct connection to the production of this book.

Dave DeVries' contribution brought this project to a new level of depth, adding both color and clarity. Tara Miller, who "does words" so well, has partnered with me through the years, putting things together in a coherent and readable fashion. Thanks also to Hugh Halter and Matt Smay, whose early collaboration helped shape the direction and scope of the project.

My gratitude to all of you who contributed the stories that helped bring the ideas to life: Colin Noyes, Keith Shields, Mark and Karen Fields, Jean-Luc Krieg, Brandon Hatmaker, Bud Simon, Caesar Kalinowski, Dana Allin, Michael Gatlin, Humberto Del Arca, and Rainer Kunz.

Thanks also to those on the publishing end: Dave Wetzler and Bob

Rummel at ChurchSmart, Carl Simmons who did the editing, Julie Becker who designed the cover, and Julia Michaud who made the layout beautiful.

It's always a terrifying thing to go through a list of names, because invariably you leave someone off. If that someone is you, please forgive me and let me know, and I'll make sure you are included in the next edition!

How can we serve you?

So having read this book, what kind of help do you need? Would you like us to come speak to your people to help them catch a vision for missional ministry? Would you like us to assist in designing a missional pilot project? Do you need guidance in creating an in-house training systems for your leaders? Do you need help with implementation? Systems restructuring? Church planter training? Missional coach training? Coaching? Would you like help equipping your people for missional living?

Both of us—Bob and Dave—do speaking, consulting, coaching, and training. We'd be glad to help you on the missional journey. You can contact us in any of the ways below.

www.missionaltoolkit.com

Bob Logan

Blog: www.loganleadership.com

Twitter: @drboblogan

Email: bob@loganleadership.com

Dave DeVries

Blog: www.missionalchallenge.com

Twitter: @davedv

Email: dave@missionalchallenge.com

Endorsements

I would highly recommend this book for anyone making a paradigm shift from models set by highly institutionalized churches, or for anyone interested in being introduced to the missional church.
> – Nick Warnes, Pastor, Northland Village Church

While the primary audience for this book is the missional church planter, network and denominational leaders will find the last chapter is worth the price of the book in itself.
> – Wayne Krause, Director, Center for Church Planting, South Pacific Division of Seventh-day Adventists

This book is an essential resource for anyone seeking to embrace an incarnational approach to mission, anyone who is looking to embrace Jesus' framework for mission.
> – Tom Johnston, Executive Director, The Praxis Center for Church Development

A great gem for established church pastors who want to catch a vision for wedding the growth and vitality of a healthy church plant with the strengths of their existing church. A combination of inspiring stories, visionary thinking, and practical strategies to transform the world.
> – The Rev. Adam T. Trambley, St. John's Episcopal Church

Taking an intentional journey, Bob has adapted his gift for systems thinking and laced it with a strong biblical foundation.
> – Joe Hernandez, Indigenous Church Planter Equipping Consultant, SBC

The most practical book on missional leadership to date.
> – Michael Bischof, President, SOULeader Resources and Lead Pastor, Tree of Life Community

Packed with easy-to-use and practical strategies that you can use right away in your ministry.
> – Roshaun Gendrett, pastor and church planter

I anticipate this will be a go-to resource in my leadership development tool box for years to come.
> – Kande Wilson, Associate Pastor, Vineyard Cincinnati

Robert Logan has 'locked-in' to the essentials of disciple-making in our present time. The principles within are transferable to new church starts as well as existing churches in need of renewed vision.
> – Dr. Sean Kelly, Sr. Pastor Peñasquitos Lutheran Church

Bob Logan… brings to this ministry a prophetic edge that is unique. If you are serious about multiplying disciples and churches that transform the world, then this book is foundational. But be careful. Bob will push you and challenge you and sometimes make you feel uncomfortable.
> – Colin Noyes, Director CoachNet Global – South Pacific

The Missional Journey is an excellent resource for understanding how to live and lead on mission.
> – Brian Howard, Director of Church Multiplication CBSC, Executive Director: Context Coaching Inc.

An invaluable, just-in-time resource for denominational leaders, pastors, church planters, and anyone serious about making and multiplying disciples.
> – Carrie Corliss, Missional network planter, Evangelical Friends Church Mid-America

Bob writes not just from the perspective of one who personally mentors strategic leaders around the globe (though he does!), but from the vantage point of one who lives what he says.
> – Dennis Bachman, Pastor of Missional Development

What I love about *The Missional Journey* is that it's not just a book, but something that you work through with other people.
> – Bob Roberts, Senior Pastor of NorthWood Church

In *The Missional Journey*, Bob Logan serves the church as an apostolic leader who shows us both the why and the way forward as the gospel is lived out through relevant missional communities.
> – Stephen Fitch, President Eden Reforestation Projects

The Missional Journey offers detailed, logical, and precise mileposts and questions needed to engage our culture with the gospel.
> – John P. Chandler, author of *Courageous Church Leadership* and leader of www.spencenetwork.org

As a network leader, this is the practical missional resource I've been looking for.
> – Dennis Jeffery, The River Conference

Bob Logan and Dave DeVries have assembled the pieces of the puzzle for church planters who are not content to just put up a sign and do church.
> – Ben Ingebretson, Church Multiplication Consultant, Reformed Church in America

The Missional Journey helps church planters and leaders ask the right questions.
> – Christina Roberts, church planter/pastor, Madison Vineyard Church

Bob has done it again. He has captured a huge, comprehensive topic like building a movement of churches into four manageable chunks.
> – Dr. Neil Tibbott, Coach for church planters and multiplication networks

Bob Logan… presents a readable, holistic approach to church planting and church development that is practical and flexible.
> – Joseph Tkach, D.Min, President, Grace Communion International

The Missional Journey demands theological rigor and discerning, prayerful work by a community. It does not offer easy programs or simple solutions. Rather, this book invites us onto a journey that leads out to new and unknown frontiers.
> – Kurt Fredrickson, DMin, PhD, Director, Doctor of Ministry Program, Fuller Theological Seminary

I have found as an evangelist that the world has shifted a great deal the last twenty years. It's time we all heed Bob Logan's direction for us and consider a new approach.
> – Doug Murren

Bob Logan's done another stellar service for the church by sharing the broad, practical implications of holistic implementation of a Kingdom-oriented, missionally-focused ministry.
> – John Wasem, US Mobilization Director for Stadia: New Church Strategies, Irvine, California

Wherever you are now, the principles Bob explores in *The Missional Journey* will help you and your community of faith more fully live into Christ's call to his people: love God, love others, make disciples!
> – Gary Diehl, Denominational Leader, The Brethren Church

Full of very practical advice and excellent questions to help you reflect and wisely chart your entire missional journey from beginning to end.
> –Michael Cadena, Director, Esperanza Para Mexico, a church growth and health coaching ministry

An excellent, comprehensive road map for the missional leader.
> – Lynda Devore, Executive Director at Our Saviour's Lutheran Church in Naperville, IL

Bob Logan has produced a guide to missional ministry so clear and user-friendly that even those of us from non-evangelical backgrounds will say: "I can do that!"
> – Rev. Kenneth F. Baker, Executive Presbyter, Presbytery of San Fernando

If you want to pick one book to read to help you connect the dots of misisonal leadership development, multiplying disciples, and multipying faith communities, I recommend this latest book by Bob Logan.
> – Rev. Dr. Brandon Cho, United Methodist pastor

The Missional Journey is a much needed call to action.
> – Dino Senesi, Lead Coach, The Senesi Group and Coach Coordinator, The Cypress Project

Some people think they must choose between impacting a culture or developing authentic Christian community. This book is a remarkably innovative road map for developing both.
> – Bob Whitesel Ph.D., author and professor of missional leadership at Wesley Seminary at Indiana Wesleyan University

For all endorsements, see www.missionaltoolkit.com.